MW00603862

APUSH Writing Guide

How to Write Winning Responses to
DBQs, LEQs, and SAQs
on the AP U.S. History Exam

Third Edition

stampede
learning systems

APUSH Writing Guide: How to Write Winning Responses to DBQs, LEQs, and SAQs on the AP U.S. History Exam (Third Edition)

Copyright © 2020 by Stampede Learning Systems.

All rights reserved. Printed in the United States of America. No part of this book may be used or reproduced in any manner without written permission from the publisher, except in the case of brief quotations embodied in critical articles or reviews.

OTHER BOOKS IN THE STAMPEDE LEARNING SERIES:

AP U.S. History Exam Prep Guide and Course Reader: Master the Most Critical Content in a Hurry

APUSH Pocket Dictionary: A Concise Reference for the AP U.S. History Exam

LIMIT OF LIABILITY / DISCLAIMER OF WARRANTY:

Stampede Learning Systems provides no guarantee as to the effect of using this book on any student's score on the AP U.S. History exam. While every effort has been made to ensure the accuracy and completeness of this work as an aid for students preparing for the AP U.S. History exam, Stampede Learning Systems does not assume any liability in connection with the information contained in this book. Stampede Learning Systems is not liable for any personal injury, property or other damages of any nature, whether special, indirect, consequential or compensatory, directly or indirectly resulting from the publication, use of, or reliance upon this book.

AP® and Advanced Placement Program are registered trademarks of the College Board, which is not affiliated with Stampede Learning Systems. The College Board was not involved in the production of, and does not sponsor or endorse, this book. All other trademarks cited in this work are the property of their respective owners.

FEEDBACK:

Should you find a factual or typographical error in this book, please report it to info@StampedeLearning.com.

Stampede Learning Systems
PO Box 44273
Milwaukee, Wisconsin 53214
www.StampedeLearning.com
info@StampedeLearning.com

ISBN: 978-0-9992794-5-8

Third Edition: 2020

CONTENTS

Introduction

SIXTY PERCENT OF THE AP U.S. HISTORY EXAM requires a written response. This creates a great opportunity for those who are proficient in writing to ensure they can pass the test. However, it may seem daunting to understand how to gain proficiency in the technical form of writing that is expected for the AP exam. Additionally, a tremendous amount of information is covered in a U.S. history course. These facts can add up to big challenges as you work through your AP class and prepare for the exam.

This guide helps simplify and speed up your exam prep process by giving you:

- **Strategies** for approaching each type of writing question on the APUSH exam: The Short Answer Question (SAQ), Long Essay Question (LEQ), and Document-Based Question (DBQ);

- **Summaries** of the events, trends, and people that are essential to know for the exam;

- **Exercises** to help you memorize important dates covered on the exam;

- **Step-by-step guidance** in how to analyze DBQ documents systematically; and

- **Practice questions** with sample answers that can be used as a model or to compare your answers to after you complete them.

The exercises and strategies in this guide will also help you in your APUSH class. But you need to put in the work; memorization takes repetition, and as with any writing technique, practice makes perfect. You also need to pace yourself so you have the chance to truly learn the material; don't try to cram.

We hope that by working through the information and exercises in this book, you will build confidence in your historical writing skills...and use those skills to ace the APUSH writing prompts!

Chapter 1
Four Crucial Tips for Tackling APUSH Writing Prompts

THE STYLE OF HISTORICAL WRITING you are expected to demonstrate on the APUSH exam is likely different from the way you are required to write for other classes. Real people read and score your APUSH writing responses – these are professional educators who are trained by the College Board to assess your mastery of historical content, analysis, and writing skills. They will examine your writing for certain characteristics, such as your ability to:

- Create a **thesis (your claim)** and defend it

- Consider **multiple points of view**

- Explain **cause and effect** relationships

- Identify **turning points** and the resulting impacts

- Describe **trends** and cite **relevant examples** that illustrate them

- Use **historical terms** appropriately

This book will help you develop all of these skills through examples and practice exercises. But knowing the information and *having* the skills is not enough – you must *demonstrate* them under the pressure of the ticking clock on exam day. And you must do so in a way that is clear, concise, and easy for the APUSH evaluator to follow. (No pressure, though.)

This chapter is devoted to a few fundamental tips you should follow to maximize your score when answering Short Answer Questions (SAQs), Long Essay Questions (LEQs), and Document-Based Questions (DBQs).

Tip 1: Write to the Rubrics

Your evaluator has only a limited amount of time to read your writing responses, so you can maximize your chances for success by focusing on the elements and approaches that are identified on the APUSH writing rubrics. While the elements of the rubrics vary by question type, in general they address the following concepts:

- **Contextualization:** Your response describes a broader historical context applicable to the prompt; that is, it explains events, developments, or processes that occurred before, during, or after the time frame referenced in the prompt.

- **Thesis / Claim:** Your response addresses the prompt with a claim and a line of reasoning that you can defend with historical information.

- **Evidence:** Your answer accurately interprets the content of the documents provided, uses additional evidence (beyond that supplied in the documents), and applies the evidence appropriately in support of your argument.

- **Analysis and Reasoning:** Your response demonstrates analytical skills as they relate to the prompt, such as explaining historical complexity, cause and effect relationships, multiple points of view, comparisons, and continuity and change over time.

There is a specific formula for how points are awarded to your response to each writing prompt. You will not earn extra points by straying from the rubrics, but you will *lose* points by failing to hit any of the required criteria. As such, it is critical that you write efficiently, taking into account the elements that are rewarded by each of the APUSH rubrics.

The rubrics vary by question type and are explained in detail in the following sections:

- *Understanding the SAQ Rubric* (page 59)

- *Understanding the LEQ Rubric* (page 75)

- *Understanding the DBQ Rubric* (page 111)

Tip 2: Look at the Verbs to Answer the Question

Respond to the question that was asked, not what you think the test writers might be getting at. This seems like an obvious point, but it bears stating. It is not unusual for students to miss the point of the question. To stay on track, one of the most useful things you can do is identify the verb. Typical verbs in essay questions are *analyze, assess, compare, evaluate,* along with the measure *to what extent.* So when you see a verb in the question, circle it and think about what the verb is instructing you to do.

- **Analyze:** Examine methodically; break down a large topic into smaller parts

- **Evaluate:** Form an opinion about the accuracy or quality of a claim; this is also a measurement of sorts and should include multiple points of view

- **Compare:** Describe the qualities that are similar and dissimilar

- **Describe:** Provide the relevant characteristics of a specified topic

- **Explain:** Use evidence or reasoning to illustrate how or why a relationship, pattern, or outcome occurs

- **Identify:** Provide information on a topic without elaboration or explanation

- **Answer "To what extent…?":** Measure the degree or magnitude of a quality or ability; you should include multiple points of view (see also: **Evaluate**)

Tip 3: Use the Years in the Question as Clues

The years specified in the questions signify important historical events. Knowing the years in which significant events occurred will help you know which events to reference in your answer. It will also help you frame your answer within the span of time between the earliest date and the latest date mentioned.

Note that you may use events that occurred before the date, and you should. By using events in your introduction or in the body paragraphs, you are giving background information. Not only does this help create a clearer image of the ideas you are discussing, it also is a method of earning a point for contextualization on the AP exam. So don't feel constrained by the initial date in the essay; it is there to help you develop a strong thesis that answers the question, but it should not completely limit the ideas you'd like to include in the essay. Additionally, you can go beyond the second date when writing your conclusion, to explain connections to other time periods. This will increase your chances of earning the complexity point. (Key dates are covered in the *Know Your Dates* chapter, starting on page 11.)

Tip 4: Make Your Thesis Easy to Find and Understand

Your thesis statement is your main answer to the LEQ and DBQ. Follow the advice below to make your thesis flow smoothly. Note that while you do not need a thesis statement for the Short Answer Questions (SAQs), you still need a strong topic sentence.

- **Do not include the dates.** The essay readers already know the dates; including them in your thesis statement usually just makes the thesis statement seem clumsy.

- **Do not rephrase the question.** You are expected to use information that you have learned to answer the question. (For more Dos and Don'ts, see the LEQ chapter on page 75 and the DBQ chapter on page 111.)

- **Do not get too specific.** Using the names of key people, events, or ideas should be reserved for the body paragraphs as evidence that your thesis has merit. Use your thesis to establish general categories and ideas that can later be supported with specific evidence in the body paragraphs of your essay. Remember: Whether it's a movie, your favorite TV show, or an essay...no one likes a spoiler.

- **Do write your thesis statement in multiple sentences.** For the LEQ, a two-sentence thesis is recommended. One sentence is allowable, but usually because the questions are complex, a one-sentence thesis statement can come across as wordy, muddled, or grammatically incorrect (e.g., a run-on sentence, or a sentence so long it's hard to tell whether the subject agrees with the verb). Additionally, if you use a two-sentence thesis, you can create a strong foundation when attempting to earn the complexity point. When writing a two-sentence thesis, look to create nuance by stating one a strong argument in the first sentence and then qualifying/identifying its limitations in the second sentence. (You will need to defend this nuance in the body of your essay.) If you do write a one-sentence thesis statement, try to accurately use a semicolon; it will help. Still, a two-sentence thesis is preferable in the LEQ because it allows you to address all parts of the question. Additionally, it can help avoid confusion when addressing two leaders, countries, eras, etc. For the DBQ, your thesis will be more complex; plan to write three to five sentences for your DBQ thesis.

- **Present a refined version of your thesis at the end of the essay.** You can earn the thesis point by providing a historically defensible claim in the introduction or conclusion of your essay. It is not uncommon for students to write a weak thesis at the beginning of their essay (which would not earn the thesis point) and to improve their thought process as the essay evolves, which allows them to write a stronger version of the thesis at the end (therefore earning the thesis point).

Chapter 2
Sample Essay Prompts by Theme

THIS CHAPTER provides examples of APUSH writing prompts, categorized by historical period or theme. Notice the verbs that start each prompt; remember the advice from *Tip 2: Look at the Verbs* (page 5) about using the verbs as a way to keep on track as you answer the question.

Settlement

- Evaluate the extent to which European settlement in the Americas changed the lifestyle of the native peoples.

- Evaluate the extent to which geography impacted the settlement of the Chesapeake and New England colonies.

- Explain the differences between settlement patterns of the Spanish, English, and French.

The American Revolution

- Evaluate the extent to which the ideas of the Enlightenment led to the outbreak of the American Revolution.

- Analyze the reasons for the patriots' victory.

The Constitution

- Evaluate the extent to which the Constitution supported the ideals of the Revolution.

- Evaluate the extent to which the Constitution resolved the problems of the Articles of Confederation.

Early Domestic Policy

- Evaluate to what extent Thomas Jefferson's election in 1800 changed the role of the federal government.

Early Foreign Policy

- Evaluate to what extent foreign aggression changed American foreign policy between 1789 and 1808.

The Market Revolution

- Evaluate to what extent the new technological innovations fostered change in the American economy from 1791 to 1848.

- Evaluate the extent to which the Market Revolution changed the United States from 1816 to 1861.

The Era of Good Feelings

- Evaluate the extent to which the Era of Good Feelings was a period of harmony in American politics.

The Reform Era

- Evaluate the extent to which the Second Great Awakening changed American life from 1800 to 1857.

Jacksonian Democracy

- Evaluate to what extent the presidency of Andrew Jackson was a turning point in American democracy.

The Antebellum Period

- Evaluate to what extent compromises were successful in reducing sectional tensions.

The Civil War

- Evaluate to what extent Northern industry was responsible for the Union victory in the Civil War.

Reconstruction

- Evaluate to what extent was the radical Reconstruction a turning point for race relations in the South.

The Gilded Age

- Evaluate to what extent railroads changed American society during the Gilded Age.

- Evaluate to what extent economic interests impacted political corruption during the Gilded Age.

- Evaluate the extent to which the Progressive Era reforms resolved the problems of the Gilded Age.

The Roaring '20s

- Evaluate to what extent World War I marked a turning point in the reform movement.

- Evaluate to what extent cultural conflicts impacted American life during the 1920s.

The Great Depression

- Evaluate to what extent the New Deal resolved the problems of the Great Depression.

World War II

- Evaluate to what extent the response of the U.S. government to authoritarian dictators reduced international tensions from 1931 to 1945.

Decades of Conservatism

- Evaluate to what extent the fears of communism impacted American society during the 1920s and the 1950s.

Post-War United States

- Evaluate to what extent the domestic policies of the U.S. government were successful following WWII. Choose two presidential administrations below to illustrate your position:
    - Harry Truman
    - Dwight Eisenhower
    - John F. Kennedy

The Cold War

- Evaluate the extent to which the failures of the Yalta Conference were responsible for the outbreak of the Cold War.

- Evaluate to what extent U.S. foreign policies were successful from 1945 to 1964.

- Evaluate to what extent U.S. foreign policies were successful from 1965 to 1980.

- Evaluate to what extent Richard Nixon's presidency was a turning point for the conservative movement in America.

The Civil Rights Movement

- Evaluate to what extent the Civil Rights movement improved life for African Americans.

- Evaluate to what extent nonviolent civil disobedience was an effective strategy for creating civil rights reforms.

- Evaluate to what extent protest movements of the 1960s influenced America's social and political climate.

- Evaluate to what extent the New Right impacted American values and legislation from 1968 to 1980.

Chapter 3
Know Your Dates

USE THE YEARS mentioned in the LEQ and DBQ prompts as hints to guide your contextualization.

The essay questions on AP exams are usually time-bound, requiring that you **limit your response to the time period identified in the question.** The years mentioned in the prompts are not arbitrary; rather, they are chosen so that you can start your essay by analyzing a specific event and end the essay with a specific event. Therefore, it is beneficial to memorize the following dates.

Later in this chapter, we provide a series of exercises for you to practice committing these dates to memory. You can find those exercises starting on page 16.

List of Key Historical Events by Year

1453	Ottoman Turks defeat Christian forces at Constantinople
1492	Columbus makes contact in the Americas
1607	Settlement of Jamestown
1620	Settlement of Plymouth
1676	Bacon's Rebellion
1680	Popé's Rebellion / Pueblo Revolt
1692-1693	Salem Witch Trials
1730s-1740s	First Great Awakening
1754	Start of the French and Indian War

1763	Proclamation of 1763
1776	American Revolution
1783	Colonists' victory in the American Revolution
	Signing of the Treaty of Paris
1786-1787	Shays' Rebellion
1787	Constitutional Convention begins
1800	Revolution of 1800
	Second Great Awakening
1803	Louisiana Purchase
	Marbury v. Madison Supreme Court decision
1812	War of 1812 begins
1815	Treaty of Ghent ends the War of 1812
1816	Tariff of 1816
1819	Panic of 1819
1820	Missouri Compromise
1820s	Market Revolution
1824	Corrupt Bargain
	Monroe Doctrine
1828	Tariff of Abominations / Nullification Crisis
1833	Compromise Tariff
1835	The Texas Revolution
1838-1839	Aroostook War
1830s	German immigration
1840s	Irish immigration
1846	Mexican War
1848	Seneca Falls Convention
	Oregon Territory acquired

1848-1855 California Gold Rush

1850 Compromise of 1850

1851 Maine Law of 1851

1854 Kansas-Nebraska Act

Ostend Manifesto

Gadsden Purchase

1854-1861 Bleeding Kansas

1856 Caning of Charles Sumner (also known as the Brooks-Sumner Affair)

1857 *Dred Scott v. Sandford* Supreme Court decision

1861-1865 Civil War

1865 Reconstruction begins

Freedmen's Bureau established

1875 Farmers' Alliance formed

1877 Compromise of 1877

1882 Chinese Exclusion Act

1896 *Plessy v. Ferguson* Supreme Court decision

1898 Spanish-American War

1914 World War I begins

1917 U.S. joins World War I

1919 Treaty of Versailles ends World War I

1922 Washington Naval Treaty (also known as the Five-Power Treaty)

1928 Kellogg-Briand Pact

1929 Stock market crash, Great Depression begins

1930s Hoovervilles built throughout the U.S.

1931 China invades Manchuria

1932 Bonus Army marches on Washington, D.C.

Stimson Doctrine

1933	Roosevelt refuses to join the London Economic Conference
	Good Neighbor Policy
1935	Italy invades Ethiopia
1935, 1936, 1937	Neutrality Acts
1936-1939	Spanish Civil War
1937	Judicial Procedures Reform Bill (also known as the Court-Packing Plan)
	Quarantine Speech
1939	World War II begins
	Cash-and-Carry Policy
1940	Destroyer Deal
1941	Lend-Lease Policy
	U.S. joins the Allies in World War II
1945	Paris Peace Treaty, World War II ends
1948	Berlin Blockade
	Berlin Airlift
1950	Korean War begins
1954	*Brown v. Board of Education* Supreme Court decision
	French defeated at Battle of Dien Bien Phu
1955	Murder of Emmett Till
	Vietnam War begins, U.S. begins supporting France in the Vietnam War
1956	Hungarian Uprising
1960	Woolworth's lunch counter sit-ins begin
1961	Bay of Pigs Invasion
	Building of the Berlin Wall
1962	Cuban Missile Crisis
1964	Civil Rights Act signed
1965	Voting Rights Act signed

1968 Martin Luther King assassinated, Civil Rights movement increases militancy

Protests at the Democratic National Convention

1972 SALT signed by Richard Nixon and Leonid Brezhnev

1973 U.S. removes troops from Vietnam

1975 Vietnam War ends

1978 Camp David Accords signed

1979 Iran Hostage Crisis begins

Practice Memorizing Dates of Key Events

To help remember the dates associated with key historical events, work through the exercises below. These exercises help you build a solid historical knowledge base by breaking down important information into manageable chunks and reinforcing it through repetition.

Directions: For each date provided, write down the event that took place in that year. Do not skip any dates within an exercise. If you cannot remember the event associated with a given date, check the *List of Key Historical Events by Year* section (page 11) or your textbook.

- **For best results, complete each exercise before moving on to the next.** Give yourself ample time between exercises; do not try to do all of them in one sitting.

The final exercise can be used as a comprehensive study aid that you should return to periodically as you get closer to the AP exam.

Exercise 1: 1453 through the 1740s

1453	_____
1492	_____
1607	_____
1620	_____
1676	_____
1680	_____
1692-1693	_____
1730s-1740s	_____

Exercise 2: 1453 through 1787

1453 _____

1492 _____

1607 _____

1620 _____

1676 _____

1680 _____

1692-1693 _____

1730s-1740s _____

1754 _____

1763 _____

1776 _____

1783 _____

_____

1786-1787 _____

1787 _____

1453 _____

1492 _____

1607 _____

1620 _____

1676 _____

1680 _____

1692-1693 _____

1730s-1740s _____

1754 _____

1763 _____

1776 _____

1783 _____

_____

1786-1787 _____

1787 _____

1800 _____

_____

1803 _____

_____

1812 _____

1815 _____

1816 _____

1819 _____

1820 _____

1820s _____

Exercise 4: 1453 through the 1840s

1453 _____

1492 _____

1607 _____

1620 _____

1676 _____

1680 _____

1692-1693 _____

1730s-1740s _____

1754 _____

1763 _____

1776 _____

1783 _____

_____

1786-1787 _____

1787 _____

1800 _____

_____

1803 _____

_____

1812 _____

1815 _____

1816 _____

1819 _____

1820 _____

1820s _____

1824 _____

_____

1828 _____

1833 _____

1835 _____

1838-1839 _____

1830s _____

1840s _____

Exercise 5: 1453 through 1861

1453 _____

1492 _____

1607 _____

1620 _____

1676 _____

1680 _____

1692-1693 _____

1730s-1740s _____

1754 _____

1763 _____

1776 _____

1783 _____
_____

1786-1787 _____

1787 _____

1800 _____
_____

1803 _____
_____

1812 _____

1815 _____

1816 _____

1819 _____

1820 _____

1820s _____

1824 _____
_____

1828 _____

1833 _____

1835 _____

1838-1839 _____

1830s _____

1840s _____

1846 _____

1848 _____

_____

1848-1855 _____

1850 _____

1851 _____

1854 _____

_____

_____

1854-1861 _____

1453 _____

1492 _____

1607 _____

1620 _____

1676 _____

1680 _____

1692-1693 _____

1730s-1740s _____

1754 _____

1763 _____

1776 _____

1783 _____

_____

1786-1787 _____

1787 _____

1800 _____

_____

1803 _____

_____

1812 _____

1815 _____

1816 _____

1819 _____

1820 _____

1820s _____

1824 _____

_____

1828 _____

1833 _____

1835 _____

1838-1839 _____

1830s _____

1840s _____

1846 _____

1848 _____

_____

1848-1855 _____

1850 _____

1851 _____

1854 _____

_____

_____

1854-1861 _____

1856 _____

1857 _____

1861-1865 _____

1865 _____

_____

1875 _____

1877 _____

Exercise 7: 1453 through 1922

1453 _____

1492 _____

1607 _____

1620 _____

1676 _____

1680 _____

1692-1693 _____

1730s-1740s _____

1754 _____

1763 _____

1776 _____

1783 _____

_____

1786-1787 _____

1787 _____

1800 _____

_____

1803 _____

_____

1812 _____

1815 _____

1816 _____

1819 _____

1820 _____

1820s _____

1824 _____

_____

1828 _____

1833 _____

1835 _____

1838-1839 _____

1830s _____

1840s _____

1846 _____

1848 _____

_____

1848-1855 _____

1850 _____

1851 _____

1854 _____

_____

_____

_____

1854-1861 _____

1856 _____

1857 _____

1861-1865 _____

1865 _____

_____

1875 _____

1877 _____

1882 _____

1896 _____

1898 _____

1914 _____

1917 _____

1919 _____

1922 _____

Exercise 8: 1453 through 1935

1453 _____

1492 _____

1607 _____

1620 _____

1676 _____

1680 _____

1692-1693 _____

1730s-1740s _____

1754 _____

1763 _____

1776 _____

1783 _____

_____

1786-1787 _____

1787 _____

1800 _____

_____

1803 _____

_____

1812 _____

1815 _____

1816 _____

1819 _____

1820 _____

1820s _____

1824 _____

_____

1828 _____

1833 _____

1835 _____

1838-1839 _____

1830s _____

1840s _____

1846 _____

1848 _____

_____

1848-1855 _____

1850 _____

1851 _____

1854 _____

_____

_____

1854-1861 _____

1856 _____

1857 _____

1861-1865 _____

1865 _____

_____

1875 _____

1877 _____

1882 _____

1896 _____

1898 _____

1914 _____

1917 _____

1919 _____

1922 _____

1928 _____

1929 _____

1930s _____

1931 _____

1932 _____

_____

1933 _____

_____

1935 _____

1453 _____

1492 _____

1607 _____

1620 _____

1676 _____

1680 _____

1692-1693 _____

1730s-1740s _____

1754 _____

1763 _____

1776 _____

1783 _____

_____

1786-1787 _____

1787 _____

1800 _____

_____

1803 _____

_____

1812 _____

1815 _____

1816 _____

1819 _____

1820 _____

1820s _____

1824 _____

_____

1828 _____

1833 _____

1835 _____

1838-1839 _____

1830s _____

1840s _____

1846 _____

1848 _____

_____

1848-1855 _____

1850 _____

1851 _____

1854 _____

_____

_____

1854-1861 _____

1856 _____

1857 _____

1861-1865 _____

1865 _____

_____

1875 _____

1877 _____

1882 _____

1896 _____

1898 _____

1914 _____

1917 _____

1919 _____

1922 _____

1928 _____

1929 _____

1930s _____

1931 _____

1932 _____

_____

1933 _____

_____

1935 _____

1935, 1936, 1937 _____

1936-1939 _____

1937 _____

_____

1939 _____

_____

1940 _____

1941 _____

_____

1945 _____

Exercise 10: 1453 through 1962

1453 _____

1492 _____

1607 _____

1620 _____

1676 _____

1680 _____

1692-1693 _____

1730s-1740s _____

1754 _____

1763 _____

1776 _____

1783 _____

_____

1786-1787 _____

1787 _____

1800 _____

_____

1803 _____

_____

1812 _____

1815 _____

1816 _____

1819 _____

1820 _____

1820s _____

1824 _____

_____

1828 _____

1833 _____

1835 _____

1838-1839 _____

1830s _____

1840s _____

1846 _____

1848 _____

_____

1848-1855 _____

1850 _____

1851 _____

1854 _____

_____

_____

1854-1861 _____

1856 _____

1857 _____

1861-1865 _____

1865 _____

_____

1875 _____

1877 _____

1882 _____

1896 _____

1898 _____

1914 _____

1917 _____

1919 _____

1922 _____

1928 _____

1929 _____

1930s _____

1931 _____

1932 _____

_____

1933 _____

_____

1935 _____

1935, 1936, 1937 _____

1936-1939 _____

1937 _____

_____

1939 _____

_____

1940 _____

1941 _____

_____

1945 _____

1948 _____

_____

1950 _____

1954 _____

_____

1955 _____

_____

1956 _____

1960 _____

1961 _____

_____

1962 _____

1453 _____

1492 _____

1607 _____

1620 _____

1676 _____

1680 _____

1692-1693 _____

1730s-1740s _____

1754 _____

1763 _____

1776 _____

1783 _____
_____

1786-1787 _____

1787 _____

1800 _____
_____

1803 _____
_____

1812 _____

1815 _____

1816 _____

1819 _____

1820 _____

1820s _____

1824 _____
_____

1828 _____

1833 _____

1835 _____

1838-1839 _____

1830s _____

1840s _____

1846 _____

1848 _____

_____

1848-1855 _____

1850 _____

1851 _____

1854 _____

_____

_____

1854-1861 _____

1856 _____

1857 _____

1861-1865 _____

1865 _____

_____

1875 _____

1877 _____

1882 _____

1896 _____

1898 _____

1914 _____

1917 _____

1919 _____

1922 _____

1928 _____

1929 _____

1930s _____

1931 _____

1932 _____

_____

1933 _____

_____

1935 _____

1935, 1936, 1937 _____

1936-1939 _____

1937 _____

_____

1939 _____

_____

1940 _____

1941 _____

_____

1945 _____

1948 _____

_____

1950 _____

1954 _____

_____

1955 _____

_____

1956 _____

1960 _____

1961 _____

_____

1962 _____

1964 _____

1965 _____

1968 _____

_____

1972 _____

1973 _____

1975 _____

1978 _____

1979 _____

Chapter 4
Framing Your Essay Responses

THIS CHAPTER PROVIDES A VARIETY OF TECHNIQUES to frame your essay responses, whether it be based on the years mentioned in the prompt, by examining themes and trends associated with certain eras, by comparing presidential administrations, or by describing the changing plight of certain groups such as women or enslaved people over time.

Using Years as Contextual Bookends

Knowing the dates of important events will help to give context when responding to SAQs, LEQs, and DBQs. This section provides some examples.

1492 through 1680

If an essay prompt on **colonization** includes the years 1492 and 1680, you should begin by discussing the arrival of **Columbus** (1492) and his **impact in Latin America.** Continue the essay by discussing the **role of the English and French** (who arrived approximately 100 years later). Finish the essay by analyzing the role of rebellions in the colonies (**Bacon's Rebellion** in 1676 and **Popé's Rebellion** in 1680).

1607 through 1693

If an essay question on **colonization** mentions the years 1607 and 1693, you should begin by discussing the economic role of **Jamestown** (1607) and compare it to the **religious reasons for settlement in New England** (1620). The question is also indicating that you should finish your essay by analyzing the **Salem Witch Trials** (1692-1693).

1754 or 1763 through 1776

Essays about the **causes of the American Revolution** often include start dates of 1754 or 1763. If the question asks you to begin in 1754, you are to discuss events during the **French and Indian War.** If the question asks you to begin in 1763, you should start your essay by analyzing the **Proclamation of 1763.** The essay question will most likely tell you to conclude your analysis in 1776 (the beginning of the **Revolution** through the **Declaration of Independence**).

1783 through 1788

If the essay is about the **creation of the American government,** you may be given a date range of 1783-1788. Begin your response with the **colonists' victory** in the American Revolution (1783). You should continue by discussing the first government of the United States, the **Articles of Confederation.** You should near completion by discussing **Shays' Rebellion** (1786-1787) and finalize your analysis by writing about the compromises and the **ratification of the U.S. Constitution.**

1803 through 1861

If an essay question asks you to analyze the **success of compromise to reduce tensions,** you will probably need to include events that occurred between 1803-1861. You should begin your essay by analyzing the effect of the **Louisiana Purchase** (1803). It's a little complex, but you could analyze the **Compromise of 1833.** You could also include the **Gag Resolutions** as a hindrance to compromise. The **Kansas-Nebraska Act** was a compromise and should definitely be included in this essay. The **caning of Charles Sumner** by Preston Brooks (1856) could be mentioned as a hindrance to compromise. You should absolutely include the *Dred Scott v. Sandford* Supreme Court decision (1857). A question that gives you the final date of 1861 is indicating that you should end your essay by analyzing the election of **Abraham Lincoln** in 1860, the **secession of South Carolina** in 1860, and the outbreak of the **Civil War** in 1861. (Hint: Since a war broke out, it would be accurate to state that, ultimately, compromise was unsuccessful.)

1812 or 1816 through the 1830s or 1840s

Questions about the **Market Revolution** often begin in 1812 or 1816. If the question asks you to begin in 1812, you should start by discussing the **War of 1812** and the **embargo** against the British. If the question asks you to begin in 1816, you should start by discussing why the United States passed the first **protective tariff.** You may discuss the role of **Samuel Slater** (textile factories, 1791) and **Eli Whitney** (cotton gin, 1793), but you need to clearly show that these developments influenced the country for several decades after they were introduced, thereby still being relevant in 1812/1816 and beyond. The question would most likely have you continue your analysis through the 1830s or 1840s. These decades are important because they show how **immigration** helped the Market Revolution grow. The **German immigrants** who came in the 1830s were essential to **farming** in the West. The **Irish immigrants** who came to America in the 1840s were influential as **industrial (factory) workers.**

1815 through 1854

Questions regarding **sectional tensions** or the **sectional balance** offer many opportunities for analysis. It is likely that there won't be time to write on all the topics within the time period provided. Events could start as early as 1815 and go as far as 1854. If this is the case, make sure you start with the first event in 1815 and end with the last event in 1854. You can pick and choose the topics you want to address between those years. The year 1815 represents the end of the **War of 1812**. At this time, the **Hartford Convention** had occurred, threatening secession in New England. This is where you want to start. Continue the essay by discussing the **Missouri Compromise** (1820). The essay could continue by analyzing the **Tariff of Abominations / Nullification Crisis,** which began in 1828 and was resolved in 1833 through the **Compromise of 1833.** After the Nullification Crisis, the next major sectional issues involved the **acquisition of territory from Mexico.** To effectively analyze this, the **Texas Revolution** (1835-1836) and the **Mexican War** (1846) should be discussed. After writing about the Mexican War you could write about the **California Gold Rush** (1848-1855); it is even more important to discuss the **Compromise of 1850.** The essay could continue with a discussion of the **Ostend Manifesto** (1854). It should wrap up with an analysis of the **Gadsden Purchase** (1854), the creation of the **Kansas-Nebraska Act** (1854) and the fighting that broke out in **Bleeding Kansas** (1854-1861).

1816 or the 1820s through 1861

Essays about the **Reform Era** often start in the 1820s (although the wording **"Antebellum period"** might be used; this refers to the period between wars, 1816-1861). In these essays, you should begin by discussing the role of the **Second Great Awakening** (1800). By covering the Second Great Awakening, you will be providing contextualization, as it is the cause of the Reform Era. Then continue with an era of reform that began in the 1820s. This could include the **abolition movement, temperance,** and **education reform.** All should be discussed, but the order is up to you based on how you want to organize your essay. You should continue by discussing the role of **Dorothea Dix** in reforming the **treatment of the mentally ill** and finish by analyzing the **women's rights movement.** You will stop in 1861, because with the outbreak of the **Civil War,** there was a break from the reform movement.

1836 through 1854

If an essay is about **Manifest Destiny,** it is likely that the starting date will be 1836. This indicates that you should begin your essay by analyzing the impact of the **Texas Revolution.** Continue by writing about the **Aroostook War** (1838-1839), and then analyze the **Mexican War** (1846). Finish by discussing the acquisition of the **Oregon Territory** (1848). Most likely the essay question will not extend beyond 1854, which allows you to discuss **attempts to expand into Cuba.**

1865 through 1877

A question about **Reconstruction** will most likely allow you to start your essay in 1865 and finish in 1877. Since 1865 is the end of the **Civil War,** you should write about the **Reconstruction Amendments** and the **Freedmen's Bureau.** Continue by analyzing the obstacles established by **Redeemer governments** in the South, such as **black codes** and **Jim Crow laws.** You can continue by discussing **military reconstruction** (troops in the South), and you should finish by discussing the end of Reconstruction which occurred through the **Compromise of 1877.**

1865 through 1900

Questions about the **Gilded Age** often begin in 1865 and end near 1900. The year 1865 marks the end of the **Civil War** and a period where there was an attempt to rebuild a divided country. The Gilded Age ended in the 1890s, which is usually considered the beginning of the **Progressive Era** (when the problems of the Gilded Age were addressed). Many interesting questions can be asked about the **American workforce** during this period. The essay should identify the challenges faced by farmers, such as railroad shipping rates (**kickbacks, rebates, pools**) and **trusts.** Problems associated with **debt** could also be discussed. Next, the farmers' proposed solutions should be examined. This will include forming groups like the **Farmers' Alliance, the Grangers,** and **the Populists.** Your essay should examine each group's strategy separately; when possible, comment on whether the goals of each group were met. After analyzing farmers, shift your focus to **factory workers.** Discuss the working conditions they endured and their causes. This will include topics such as **immigration, political machines,** and **trusts.** You will also want to address the federal government's **laissez-faire** economic policy. After describing the **working conditions,** identify and explain how workers tried to address those conditions. Include the major **labor unions** such as the **NLU,** the **Knights of Labor,** and the **AFL.** Be sure to comment on whether or not each union's goals were met.

1890s through 1921

If you have a question that begins in the 1890s and ends in 1921, it is most likely asking about the **Progressive Era.** You should begin with the contributions of the **muckrakers.** Then continue with progressive measures that occurred in the early 1900s administration. This can include **federal improvements** (Teddy Roosevelt's **Square Deal**), and it can include **municipal improvements** and **state improvements.** The order doesn't matter as long as you organize your ideas effectively. You may also discuss court cases like *Lochner v. New York* and *Muller v. Oregon.* Continue with an analysis of the **Triangle Shirtwaist Factory fire.** You could address organizations that were created like the **Sierra Club** and the conflicts that arose between **preservationists** and **conservationists.** Then analyze the presidency of **William Howard Taft.** Focus on his **trust busting.** The final topics for analysis should include the presidency of **Woodrow Wilson** and his attacks on the "**triple wall of privilege**," as well as the passage of the 19th Amendment which gave women the right to vote.

The 1920s

The 1920s was a decade in which American society was involved in many **social conflicts.** As a result, questions on this decade often ask you to explain why this happened and to analyze the outcome of these clashes. One topic that should be included is the conflicts between religion and science (**Scopes Monkey Trial**). There were also challenges between **religious beliefs** and the **use of birth control.** Fears of **communism** (**Red Scare, A. Mitchell Palmer**) clashed with new ideas on economics and government. There were debates over **immigration** (the **Emergency Quota Act,** the **National Origins Act**). There was also a resurgence in **racial prejudice** (the **KKK,** the film *The Birth of a Nation*) and attempts by African Americans to achieve equality (**Marcus Garvey,** the **Harlem Renaissance**).

1929 through 1945

Questions about the **Great Depression** or evaluating **the success of the New Deal** often start in 1929 when the stock market crashed on **Black Tuesday.** The essay should continue by evaluating the policies of **Herbert Hoover**'s presidency, like the **Reconstruction Finance Corporation,** the creation of **Hoovervilles** (1930s), and the **Bonus Army**'s march on Washington, D.C. (1932). After evaluating Hoover's presidency, the focus should turn to President **Franklin Roosevelt** and his banking reforms and job creation during his **First 100 Days** (1933). As Roosevelt's presidency continues, write about failures in his **New Deal** (consider policies that were found unconstitutional by the Supreme Court). The **Court-Packing Plan** (1937) will also need to be discussed. Finally, ensure that the response includes analysis of **WWII** and a clear explanation of how the war brought the U.S. out of the Great Depression.

1919 through 1941

Two very similar questions can begin with the Treaty of Versailles in 1919. A great way to approach the introduction to an essay question asking about the **causes of World War II** would be to begin with the **Treaty of Versailles.** The thesis and the first body paragraph should begin with events as early as 1931; this date indicates the Japanese invasion of **Manchuria.** The international response (or lack thereof) should be investigated in this section of your essay as well. Continue by analyzing the policies used by the U.S. government to remain **neutral.** It is also advantageous to combine American policies with an analysis of the European policy of **appeasement.** Continue with the war breaking out in Europe (1939) and U.S. policies like **Cash-and-Carry** (1939), the **Destroyer Deal** (1940), and the **Lend-Lease Policy** (1941), all of which **abandoned neutrality.** The essay should end in 1941 when the Japanese attacked **Pearl Harbor** and the U.S. officially entered the war on the side of the **Allies.**

The Treaty of Versailles can also be a starting point for explaining **how American foreign policy changed after WWI.** Despite President Wilson's goals, the U.S. government took all possible measures to become **isolationist.** Evidence from the 1920s includes refusal to join the **League of Nations,** the **Five-Power Treaty** (also known as the **Washington Naval Treaty,** 1922), the **Kellogg-Briand** Pact (1928), and the creation of **high tariffs.** The U.S. continued to try to be isolationist in the early 1930s. This can be shown through the **Stimson Doctrine** (1932), FDR's refusal to join the **London Economic Conference** (1933), planning for **Filipino independence,** and **recognition of the Russian (communist) government.** FDR also tried to reduce the threat of the spread of fascism by instituting the **Good Neighbor Policy** (1933). It would be useful to analyze the international threats that continued to occur in the 1930s, such as **German militarization, Mussolini's attack on Ethiopia** (1935), and treaties that should have been of concern. In response, the U.S. continued to remain neutral (**Johnson Debt Default Act, Neutrality Acts** of 1935, 1936, 1937, and the **Spanish Civil War,** 1936-1939). Even when FDR wanted to start to reduce Japanese expansion (**Quarantine Speech,** 1937), he was rejected. European nations followed the practice of **appeasement** until they had no choice but to go to war. Finally, that led to the U.S. abandoning neutrality through the **Neutrality Act of 1939.** (See also the specifics mentioned in the previous paragraph.)

1945 through 1991

If the dates range from 1945-1991, the question will most likely be dealing with the **Cold War,** since 1945 marks the **end of World War II.** Therefore, the essay should begin with the **end of the alliance** between the U.S. and the Russians during the war. Early ideas should include **containment,** the **Truman Doctrine,** and the **Marshall Plan.** These ideas should be used when analyzing **Greece, Turkey,** and **Germany (Berlin)** during the late 1940s. It could include the creation of **NATO** and the **Korean War.** In the 1950s, areas for analysis could include **French-Indochina/domino theory,** the **coup in Iran,** the **Hungarian Uprising,** and/or the **Suez Crisis.** In the 1960s, topics could include Kennedy's investment in the **space race,** the **Berlin Wall,** the **Bay of Pigs Invasion,** and/or the **Cuban Missile Crisis.** There should also be continued analysis of President Kennedy's and President Johnson's policy of **escalation** in Vietnam. During Nixon's presidency of the late '60s and early '70s, **Vietnamization** should be discussed. Also, the policy of **détente** must be analyzed. If you have time, you could write about the failure of **SALT II** under President Carter. The essay should near its end with President Reagan and the **Star Wars/SDI** program. The final analysis of the essay should include the **fall of the Berlin Wall** and Mikhail Gorbachev's implementation of **glasnost** and **perestroika,** which ended the Cold War.

1946 through 1968

Essay questions about **civil rights** could start as early as 1946 when President **Harry Truman** created an executive order to **desegregate the military.** However, it is not uncommon for the question to start in 1954. If that is the case, the information about Truman would work very well in the introduction. The early analysis of the thesis and the early body paragraphs should focus on civil rights during **Dwight Eisenhower**'s presidency. The reason essay questions begin with the date 1954 is because the question is asking you to start your analysis with the Supreme Court's decision in *Brown v. Board of Education.* It is logical to continue by discussing the **Little Rock Nine** (1957). It would also be worthwhile to analyze the murder of **Emmett Till** and the **Montgomery Bus Boycott** (1955). The **Woolworth's lunch counter sit-ins** could also be discussed. During **John F. Kennedy**'s presidency of the 1960s, you could focus on the **Freedom Rides,** the **voter education project, James Meredith,** and actions of **nonviolent civil disobedience** led by **Martin Luther King, Jr.** It is also important to analyze the murder of **Medgar Evers** and the terrorist **bombing of the 16th Street Baptist Church** in Birmingham, Alabama. After the **assassination of JFK,** it is necessary to discuss the **Civil Rights Act of 1964** and the **Voting Rights Act of 1965** signed by President Lyndon Johnson. The second half of the essay should focus on the **militant phase** of the Civil Rights movement. Some of the following groups should be analyzed: **The Nation of Islam, The Black Panthers, Black Power.** The **Watts Riot** could also be discussed.

The 1950s through the 1970s

It is possible that a more general essay question could ask you to focus on several of the **social movements** of the 1950s, 1960s, and 1970s which were aimed at improving the rights of various groups. In addition to the information on the **Civil Rights movement** (mentioned earlier), you could also discuss the **Free Speech movement** which began at the University of California, Berkeley in 1964. It would be logical to continue with the **SDS** and its stance on **civil liberties,** the **Vietnam War, women's rights,** and **economic injustice.** You could continue your essay with a brief analysis of the **Weathermen.**

Connecting Historical Periods with Trends

It is important to be able to connect certain decades, periods, and presidencies with trends in the United States. Examples are provided below.

Treatment of Indians During the Colonial Period

If asked a question about the treatment of Indians during the colonial period, the **Spanish** treated the Indians brutally and exploited them through mining and farming for **cash crops (encomienda system)**. The Spanish also **forcibly assimilated** the Indians and **intermarried** and created a new social structure. The **English** did not put much effort into assimilation (one of the few attempts were the **praying towns**). Instead the English tried to **drive the Indians off the land.** The **French worked with the Indians** when trapping. They also **traded** with the Indians which *indirectly* **led to assimilation.** The French also **intermarried** with Indian women, but they did not create a hierarchy like the Spanish had.

Similarities and Differences Between the Gilded Age and the 1920s

The Gilded Age and the 1920s were similar in several ways. This allows for an essay question to ask about the similarities and differences of these two periods. Both time periods were known for **political corruption.** Also, many Americans were **anti-immigrant.** However, there were a few notable people who helped and supported immigrants even though it was not a popular position. During both periods, **science** challenged traditional **religious beliefs (Darwin/evolution, Scopes/teaching evolution)**. Government supported **business over labor** during both periods as well and **did not help farmers** when they needed assistance from the government. During both periods, the U.S. followed an **isolationist** foreign policy. Additionally, the eras following the Gilded Age and the Roaring '20s were both periods of government intervention. A major difference between the two periods is that in the 1920s, the artistic contributions of African Americans were recognized through the **Harlem Renaissance**, whereas they were ignored in the Gilded Age. Another difference was that women could not vote during the Gilded Age; they finally gained the right to vote in 1920. (However, it must be noted that women still had to fight for equal rights during and after the 1920s.)

Similarities and Differences Between the 1920s and 1950s

In many ways the decades of the 1920s and 1950s were similar. An essay question could ask you to compare the two decades. If you are asked to compare the two decades you should focus on the **anti-union sentiment** and the **government support of business** during both eras. Both decades were also times of great **consumerism;** both were aided by new forms of **technology**, the radio and the TV. Note that while consumerism was not sustainable in the 1920s, it was in the 1950s. Both decades were periods when **women** advocated for more independence and **African Americans** fought for **equal rights.** Also, both decades were times of **scientific inquiry** (**Scopes Trial** in the 1920s; **space and aeroscience** in the 1950s). Although there were many similarities, the **foreign policy** was completely different. The 1920s was a decade of **isolation** (disillusionment from WWI), whereas the 1950s was a decade of **intervention** (**Cold War** fears about the spread of communism).

Similarities and Differences Between the New Deal and the Great Society

FDR's **New Deal** and LBJ's **Great Society** had similar goals; this was because Johnson had wanted to expand the goals of the New Deal during his presidency. For this reason, it is not uncommon to be asked to compare the two plans. Franklin Roosevelt's New Deal focused on helping **average citizens,** whom he referred to as the **"forgotten man."** To achieve his goal of improving life for the American people, he initiated **reforms in banking and finance,** created jobs to **reduce unemployment,** and tried to pass legislation that would assist farmers. FDR also helped the elderly by implementing **Social Security** benefits. Lyndon Johnson created a plan called **The Great Society,** which aimed to eliminate institutionalized racism (**Civil Rights** and **Voting Acts**) and **eradicate poverty.** Poverty was addressed through legislation like the **Economic Opportunity Act,** which created jobs, and several other acts to improve educational opportunities. Additionally, LBJ made improvements to healthcare through **Medicare** and **Medicaid** and **expanded Social Security** benefits. A major difference between their administrations was that FDR was largely unable to pass legislation that would improve the condition of African Americans due to opposition from Southern Democrats, whereas Johnson was able to pass the **Civil Rights Act of 1964** and the **Voting Rights Act of 1965.**

Civil Rights Reform Efforts of 1890-1920s Compared to the 1950s-1960s

Occasionally you may be asked to write an essay that compares the efforts to improve civil rights from 1890 through the 1920s and the Civil Rights movement of the 1950s and 1960s. The first period should focus on people like **Booker T. Washington (economic equality)** and **W.E.B. DuBois (complete equality** starting with the **Talented Tenth**). The essay could continue with the attempts by the **KKK** to use terror to threaten Black people from seeking better treatment. Information about the **Harlem Renaissance** could be used to show the success of Black culture in overcoming racist forms of entertainment such as the film *The Birth of a Nation* or the first talkie *The Jazz Singer.* The efforts for improved civil rights in the 1920s should conclude with an analysis of **Marcus Garvey**'s ideas. The 1950s and 1960s should focus on the information given earlier. You could begin as early as 1946 to add context, and you should end your analysis with the events of 1968. You will have to be selective in which information you feel best complements the information from the 1890s through the 1920s, since there will not be enough time to write about everything listed.

Comparing Presidencies from 1948 through the 1980s

It is possible that you will be asked to compare various presidencies from 1948 through the 1980s. As a result, it would be beneficial to understand the similarities and differences of the presidential administrations from Truman through Reagan. It is highly unusual for a DBQ prompt to extend beyond 1980; an LEQ prompt, on the other hand, will always allow you to select an option that requires analysis of events up to the present day. As such, it doesn't hurt to learn the information about more recent presidencies provided in your textbook or in class as well.

Truman

Truman's **Fair Deal** attempted to spread affluence equally throughout society. It also sought to improve **civil rights,** create **affordable housing,** and extend **education.** In addition, the Truman Administration wanted to provide **universal healthcare,** help **labor unions,** and assist **veterans.**

Eisenhower

Eisenhower's domestic policy, **Modern Republicanism,** wanted to strike a balance between too much government involvement while still ensuring Americans had a **limited governmental safety net.** During his presidency, he opposed federal funding to **public schools** and **universal healthcare,** yet he expanded **Social Security** benefits, increased the **minimum wage,** and increased government funding of **public housing.**

Kennedy

Kennedy's **New Frontier** plan attempted to eliminate poverty by **increasing unemployment and Social Security benefits** and the **minimum wage,** and by **expanding public housing.** Additionally, legislation he signed helped **farmers** and the **environment.** Kennedy also supported **civil rights** and **women's equality.** Regarding foreign policy, he supported **arms control** and **disarmament** while strengthening **special operations units** in the military.

Nixon

Nixon's domestic policy, **New Federalism,** turned over key federal responsibilities to states, believing that **state government** was closer to the people and, therefore, could more effectively meet the needs of its residents. This was done by giving states **block grants.** While Nixon stated he wanted to create a smaller, less costly government, he added to the scope and costs of the federal government by increasing **Social Security, Medicare,** and **Medicaid.** Although he attempted to make changes to **welfare,** he was unsuccessful. Nixon also ended the **busing program** that had been created to desegregate schools. Although many in the environmental movement criticized Nixon, legislation to protect the **environment** was also passed during his presidency. Regarding foreign policy, Nixon was successful at establishing **détente** and pursued a policy of **Vietnamization** to limit U.S. involvement in the Vietnam War.

Carter

Carter responded to high petroleum prices by passing the **Emergency Gas Act** and creating the **Department of Energy.** To reduce the need for oil, the Carter Administration also passed Corporate Automobile Fuel Efficiency **(CAFE) standards,** which improved fuel efficiency of automobiles. During Carter's presidency, the **Three Mile Island disaster** occurred, illustrating the dangers of **nuclear power** and reducing public support for nuclear energy. Carter advocated for **environmental issues.** When toxic waste dumps were uncovered, he created the **EPA Superfund,** which allowed the government to clean up hazardous waste. **Stagflation,** which had begun during the Nixon administration, worsened during Carter's presidency. In foreign policy, Carter was successful at reducing tension between the Egyptians and Israelis through the **Camp David Accords.** However, Carter had limited success in his **SALT II** agreement with Soviet leader Leonid Brezhnev. Although they agreed to have equal amounts of nuclear weapons, the agreement did little to reduce the arms race. Carter's biggest foreign policy failure occurred during the **Iranian Hostage Crisis** when he was unable to secure the release of the American hostages.

Reagan

Reagan attempted to improve the faltering U.S. economy through across-the-board tax cuts. Reagan believed in **supply-side economics (Reaganomics),** and as a result, most of the tax cuts went to large businesses. To offset the loss in revenue, Reagan cut benefits to **social welfare programs** such as **Social Security, Medicaid,** and **Food Stamps.** Federal funding of **public education** dropped precipitously, and he also **reduced funding for the EPA.** Although these cuts were meant to save the government money, **military spending** increased dramatically. Reagan believed that although the military spending was high and tax revenue was lower, the U.S. could avoid a growing deficit through business expansion created by his tax cuts. Reagan declared a **"War on Drugs,"** which led to skyrocketing incarceration of nonviolent drug offenders. He also attacked **labor unions,** most notably during the Professional Air Traffic Controllers Organization **(PATCO)** strike, in which he fired all of the workers who were on strike. Regarding foreign policy, Reagan used strong rhetoric to attack **communism.** Additionally, during his presidency the **Iran-Contra scandal** occurred during which the military illegally sold weapons to the Iranians and funneled the money to the Contra rebels, attempting to overthrow the leftist government of Nicaragua.

Understanding the Path of Key Groups Throughout History

You may be asked about certain groups throughout history. It will be important to identify trends and turning points for these groups.

Women

During the **colonial period** (1607-1776), women did not have many rights. They were **not allowed to vote** (even if they were members of a church). Additionally, Northern women had **no property rights.** Because there were so few women in the South, they were allowed to own property. In both cases, women were expected to **stay at home** and **raise the children.** Women were also viewed as weaker and more easily corruptible. During the **Salem Witch Trials,** 144 women were accused of being witches, compared to only 44 men.

During the **Revolutionary period** (1776-1783), women were helpful in the movement for **independence.** They served as nurses, seamstresses, and cooks. Occasionally women joined in the fighting, as well. **Margaret Corbin** was tasked with loading the cannon while her husband fired it. After he was killed during battle, she took his place and continued firing until she was wounded. Other women, like **Deborah Sampson,** disguised themselves as men so that they would be allowed to serve in the military in a combat role. When the war was over, **Abigail Adams** wrote a letter to her husband to **"remember the ladies."** However, women did not obtain political rights (voting/property). Instead, the concept of **republican motherhood** kept them in the home to teach their children civic virtue. Some historians argue that this was an elevation of their station. However, it is important to note that women did not benefit politically or economically; in fact, not being able to work outside the home left them completely dependent on their husbands.

During the **Second Great Awakening** (early 1800s), women became valued for their **spiritual worth.** Beginning in the 1820s, they began to get involved in reform movements like **abolition, temperance,** and the **treatment of the mentally ill.** They also began to advocate for themselves and assert that they should have **equal rights.** Although women were advocating for themselves, they still faced obstacles. They were allowed to work in factories during the Market Revolution if they were single. As a result, single women had a measure of economic independence. However, when they got married, women were expected to be a part of the **Cult of Domesticity** by leaving their jobs and **staying in the home to raise their children** and **guide their husbands to observe moral values.** The high point of this period was the **Seneca Falls Convention** in 1848. However, as the Civil War approached, the women's rights movement was paused.

During **Reconstruction** (1865-1877), women's rights were wholly overlooked. The **14ᵗʰ and 15ᵗʰ Amendments** both gave rights to the freedmen, but women did not have protection of their civil rights or voting rights.

Women continued to struggle for equality — specifically **voting rights** — during the **Gilded Age.** (1865-1900). They were able to continue working as reformers through the **Settlement Houses.** This reignited women's activism and desire for **social reform** (which included women's rights). To achieve their goal of suffrage, the National American Women Suffrage Association (**NAWSA**) was created. **New opportunities in employment** also helped women gain independence. However, unless they were poor, women were still expected to return to the home when married.

The women's rights movement continued to move forward in **the 1920s.** Due to their contributions on the home front during WWI, the **19ᵗʰ Amendment** was passed, giving women the right to vote. Additionally, women like **Margaret Sanger** tried to increase women's freedom outside of the home by advocating for the use of **birth control. Alice Paul** campaigned for an **Equal Rights Amendment** which would guarantee women equal treatment. Also, **flappers** challenged traditional concepts of ladylike behavior by changing their fashion, drinking, and smoking, showing that they would not follow traditional gender roles.

World War II also caused women to **work in factories** to help the wartime economy. This showed women could be mothers and work outside of the house. In the post-war period, many women went back to the home with the **baby boom,** while other women continued to work. Even though women found employment opportunities after the war, the workplace was not equal. **Betty Friedan** became a leading voice amongst feminists to try to improve the lives of women. This led to the National Organization for Women (**NOW**), which championed an Equal Rights Amendment (**ERA**) and **Title IX.** Women also gained more control over their reproductive decisions through the Supreme Court decision in *Roe v. Wade.*

Enslaved People

There may also be essay questions that refer to **enslaved people's resistance** against the oppression of slavery. It is important to realize that there were many ways that enslaved people resisted, most of which were **nonviolent.** They included strategies such as **work slowdowns, pretending to be sick,** and taking an **extra-long time to heal** if they were beaten or whipped. They also resisted through their **religious beliefs.** Enslaved people kept elements of their **African culture** in their religious practices. In addition, the sections of the Bible that they emphasized dealt with resistance to slavery and being led to freedom (Exodus). They also resisted by **running away (Underground Railroad).** Least frequent, but still vitally important to analyze, are the **rebellions of enslaved people (Stono, Nat Turner, Denmark Vesey).**

Immigrants and Migrants

There are many eras in which movement could be analyzed. This includes immigration and migration. **Early immigration** to America could begin during the 17th century. This would focus primarily on the **English** who were immigrating to the **South for economic reasons** and to **New England for religious reasons.** In this situation, it might be useful to show that a **social class system** existed in each section of the country. In the South, it was based on **wealth;** in the North, it was based on **church membership.**

A discussion of immigration in the **1830s and 1840s** should focus on the **Old Immigrants (Germans** and **Irish).** The **Germans immigrated in the 1830s** because they wanted to live in a democratic nation. The majority of the Germans were not poor and, as a result, could afford to **move west and work as farmers.** They did not face brutal discrimination; however, they were looked down upon because they did not hold the sabbath to the same sacred level as the native Christians. **The Irish immigrated in the 1840s** in response to the **potato famine.** The Irish were poor and, as a result, could not move beyond the cities that they arrived in when immigrating. This led to large Irish populations which threatened the **nativists.** The threat was **economic (job competition), political (political machines/voting blocs),** and **social** (fear that **Catholicism** would become the dominant religion). As a result, the nativists were strongly prejudiced against the Irish, and nativist organizations were created in opposition to the Irish immigrants.

The **New Immigrants** began arriving in America during the **Gilded Age up to the 1920s.** They included Southern and Eastern European immigrants from **Italy, Poland,** and **Russia.** The Eastern European immigrants were hated for many of the same reasons the Irish were hated a generation earlier. To reduce the impact of New Immigrants, the **Emergency Quota Act** (1921) was created; immigration restrictions were made even stronger by the **National Origins Act** (1924). During this period, there was also an influx of immigrants from **China** and **Japan.** The Chinese had done much of the farm labor until 1882 when the **Chinese Exclusion Act** banned any more Chinese from entering the United States. The Japanese also took jobs in farm labor until 1908, when the **Gentlemen's Agreement** stopped Japanese immigration.

An internal migration, the **Great Migration,** occurred during and shortly after World War I. Hundreds of thousands of **Black Southerners came to the North** for the economic opportunities that existed by **working in factories** compared to sharecropping in the South. They also moved to escape the deep **racism** that still existed in the South. Racism still existed in the North. After WWI ended, **competition over jobs and housing** led to violent **race riots.** The movement also had a cultural impact as the **Harlem Renaissance** occurred in New York.

During **WWII,** a second internal migration occurred, also known as the Great Migration (or the **Second Great Migration**). The cause of this migration was similar to the reasons of the migration during WWI. The effects were also similar; racism connected with housing led many white families to leave the cities, a phenomenon known as **"white flight,"** which led to **growth of suburbs** and **urban decay** in the cities.

Mexican immigrants had been doing farm work in the United States since the early 1900s; however, there is typically a stronger focus on **Mexican immigration during WWII.** During the war, the **Bracero Program** was created to fill the farm worker shortage that occurred when American soldiers went to fight in Europe. Once WWII was over, the U.S. wanted to reduce the number of Mexican migrants into the nation. This desire was strengthened in 1965 with the **Immigration and Nationality Act,** which set strict **quotas** for the number of people who could immigrate from Latin American countries.

There are also notable changes regarding **Asian immigrants** in the **post-WWII** period. Some soldiers who had been stationed in Asia had been involved in relationships with Asian women. As a result, new laws were passed with allowed these **Asian brides, fiancées,** and **adopted children** to immigrate to the United States. Immigration for **Filipinos** also became much easier after the war. In 1952 and 1965, new laws eliminated all former legislation that allowed discrimination of immigrants based on quotas or their ethnicity.

Chapter 5
All About Short Answer Questions
(SAQs)

Anatomy of an SAQ

Each Short Answer Question (SAQ) asks you to respond to a two-part or three-part prompt. Some Short Answer Questions start with a brief reading (quotations or background material) to set the stage for the two- or three-part question.

There are three Short Answer Questions that each have two or three parts, so **you will be answering a total of up to nine questions in 40 minutes.** This means that for each individual question asked [i.e., 1 (a), 1 (b), and 1 (c)], you should average approximately four minutes for reading and responding.

To avoid overlapping your answers for any parts of the question [i.e., 1 (a), 1 (b), or 1 (c)], **read all parts of the question before answering any one part of the question.**

Understanding the SAQ Rubric

The rubric used by exam evaluators to award points for SAQs is much more straightforward than those used for LEQs and DBQs. Its focus is quite simply: Did you fully and accurately answer the questions asked?

3 Points	Response accomplishes all three tasks set by the question
2 Points	Response accomplishes two of the tasks set by the question
1 Point	Response accomplishes one of the tasks set by the question
0 Points	Response accomplishes none of the tasks set by the question

Tips for Tackling SAQs

Tip 1: Think Inside the Box

It is incredibly important to note that **you may use only one page to answer** all three parts of a Short Answer Question.

Each SAQ response page features a box containing 23 lines where you should write your answer. Keep your answer inside the box. **Any writing outside the box on the page will NOT be scored.**

Tip 2: Divide and Conquer

A good strategy to ensure that you write enough, but not too much, is to **divide the answer sheet into three sections.** Make small placemarks on the right and left side of your paper one-third of the way down the page (7 lines) and two-thirds (15 lines) of the way down the page.

This will help you know approximately how much space you have to answer all parts of the question equally. Placing these small marks in the margins gives you a guideline that you can adhere to, but it also allows you to write a little further if necessary.

But remember: Your entire answer must fit within the box.

While some students choose to label their answers **(a), (b),** and **(c),** there is no requirement that this be done. In fact, it may be beneficial not to "tell" the AP readers who score your exam which part of the question you are intending to answer.

This is because you may not completely cover the answer to **(a)** in the top segment of your paper, but you might finish your thought in the middle or bottom segment.

If you label each part of your answer by letter, the reader will not give you a point for finally getting around to completing your response to **(a)** in the section labeled **(c)**. On the other hand, if you do **not** label your short response sections by letter, the reader must give you the benefit of the doubt and give you the point.

If you feel it is necessary to label your response by letter to help you answer all three prompts, **use your pen to scratch out the letters after you have finished answering the question.**

Tip 3: Start with a Clear Statement that Answers the Question (No Thesis Required)

Like the LEQ and DBQ, you are required to stay within a time frame or historical period when you respond to Short Answer Questions. Unlike the LEQ and DBQ, **you do not need a thesis.**

The key to writing a strong response to the Short Answer Question is to start by **clearly answering the question that is being asked** and then to **use evidence throughout your response** that supports your answer.

Tip 4: Lean on the Reading (But Not Too Much)

There may be times where you will get the entire answer from a selected reading given in the question. Use your reading skills and critical thinking ability to **find the answer in the reading.**

Also, **make sure the answer is in your own words** (you may even be able to add a little information from what you have learned in class). DO NOT rewrite the differing perspectives as they are presented in the selected reading accompanying the question.

Tip 5: Show the Right Evidence

To ensure your answers are strong, you must provide evidence. This can usually be done by answering the questions **"Why?"** or **"How?"**

- Why was an event significant?

- Why did an event signal a turning point?

- How did a historical figure's decision affect future events?

- How was a historical figure's decision viewed by others?

Once you have answered the questions of "Why?" or "How?", include a more detailed description to provide evidence that your position has merit.

Practice Responding to Short Answer Questions

This section provides four sample Short Answer Questions, space for you to write a response, and a sample of a well-written response for each question.

Write your answer to the practice question before reading the sample answer. By comparing your response to a model answer, you can identify similarities and differences and find ways to improve your own answer next time.

Exercise 12: Short Answer Practice Question 1

SAQ 1 Prompt

Answer parts (a), (b), and (c).

  (a) Briefly explain ONE important similarity between Spanish settlement and British settlement.

  (b) Briefly explain ONE important difference between Spanish settlement and British settlement.

  (c) Briefly explain ONE factor that accounts for the difference you indicated in **(b)**.

Write a Response to SAQ 1

Note: After completing your answer, we recommended you scratch out the letters (a), (b), and (c).

(a) The Spanish and the British both had a desire to profit from cash crops grown in the Americas. The Spanish created encomiendas where Indians were forced to help raise crops that could be sold in Europe. The British set up their first permanent colony in Jamestown, where John Rolfe discovered that tobacco could be cultivated and sold for a profit. (b) The Spanish focused on converting Indians, whereas the English had no real interest in conversion. The Spanish had begun to strengthen Christianity through the Reconquista and desired to continue to make it the dominant religion throughout the world. As a result, they were focused on converting the Indians. This could be seen through the Battle of Acoma when they fought the Pueblos to force them to assimilate. It could also be seen through the series of missions that Fr. Junipero Serra created in California. The English had little interest in converting the Indians. There were no attempts made in the Chesapeake; rather, the British drove Indians like the Powhatans off the land. In New England, there were limited and weak attempts to convert Indians in praying towns; however, those weak attempts were abandoned after King Philip's War. (c) Along with the impact of the Reconquista, the Spanish men that came to the Americas typically came alone. As a result, they married native women and had children creating a new race, mestizos. The Spanish had their wives convert to Catholicism and raised their children as Catholic. The English who settled in New England came primarily with their families. As a result, they did not need to intermarry and, therefore, did not spread their religion to the Indians living near them.

Exercise 13: Short Answer Practice Question 2

Source Material

"Few, if any, occasions within the past thirty years have meant more to the Negro race than that which calls us here. The Negro has been a laborer in this country nearly three hundred years, but with few exceptions he has been a forced laborer, an unskilled laborer, or an ignorant laborer; but here at the mouth of the James ... we have inaugurated today the largest and most complete attempt in this country to make the Negro an intelligent, conscientious, skillful producer, and to have him appreciate the dignity, beauty, and civilizing power that there is in labor."

— Booker T. Washington, Address delivered at the Hampton Institute

"Easily the most striking thing in the history of the American Negro since 1876 is the ascendancy of Mr. Booker T. Washington.... Mr. Washington came, with a single definite programme.... His programme of industrial education, conciliation of the South, and submission and silence as to civil and political rights, was not wholly original;... But Mr. Washington first indissolubly linked these things; he put enthusiasm, unlimited energy, and perfect faith into this programme, and changed it from a by-path into a veritable Way of Life."

— W.E.B. Du Bois, "Of Mr. Booker T. Washington and Other," *The Souls of Black Folks*

SAQ 2 Prompt

Using the excerpts above, answer (a), (b), and (c).

(a) Briefly describe ONE significant difference between Booker T. Washington's methods for improving the position of African Americans and W.E.B. Du Bois's method.

(b) Briefly explain how ONE significant historical event or development could have supported Booker T. Washington's position.

(c) Briefly explain how ONE significant historical event or development could have supported W.E.B. Du Bois's position.

Write a Response to SAQ 2

Sample Response to SAQ 2

Note: After completing your answer, we recommended you scratch out the letters (a), (b), and (c).

(a) Booker T. Washington believed that African Americans could improve their condition by focusing on economic improvement, specifically learning skilled trades, as a result he created the Tuskegee Institute. W.E.B. Du Bois thought that Washington was an accommodationist and was critical of Washington's strategy. Du Bois thought that immediate social and political equality should be given to African Americans and it should begin with the "talented 10%," a group he believed could prove to the nation that Black citizens were equally capable as white citizens in all areas of life. (b) Black Southerners had struggled economically after the Civil War. Laws like the black codes prevented them from owning or renting land. Without any other employable skills, the freedmen had no choice but to work as sharecroppers, often for the same men who had been their former masters. Working as a sharecropper left most Southern Black people in poverty. As a result, Booker T. Washington saw becoming a skilled laborer as a way out of this system of exploitation. (c) W.E.B. Du Bois focused on other developments like the creation of the Jim Crow laws. Before these laws were implemented, freedmen had success through organizations like the Union League, voting and electing Black candidates into office. However, with the implementation of Jim Crow laws which created a poll tax and literacy tests, Black people in the South were prevented from voting, which ensured that racist redeemer governments would remain in control and civil and political rights of Black Americans would be ignored regardless of the 14th and 15th Amendments.

Exercise 14: Short Answer Practice Question 3

SAQ 3 Prompt

U.S. historians have proposed various events to mark the origin of the Civil War. Address parts (a) and (b) in your response.

(a) Choose one of the events below and explain why your choice best represents the origins of the Civil War. Provide at least one piece of evidence to support your position.

- The Mexican War

- The Kansas-Nebraska Act

- The Dred Scott Decision

(b) Explain why your choice is better than another option.

Write a Response to SAQ 3

Sample Response to SAQ 3

Note: After completing your answer, we recommended you scratch out the letters (a), (b), and (c).

(a) The Mexican War was when the Civil War originated. Before the Mexican War, there had been the ability to create compromises that were followed by both sections of the country such as the Missouri Compromise. However, the land gained from Mexico created new debates that could not be solved through compromise. Although the Compromise of 1850 was created, it could not satisfy either section of the country, and as a result, it was not honored. This was clear when Northerners would not follow the fugitive slave law and Southerners were outraged that they were losing control of the sectional balance evident through the votes cast for free soil in the new territories. This initial conflict led to a series of other disputes, but all of them originate with the conflict over the Mexican War and the Compromise of 1850. (b) Because the South was losing the sectional balance, there was a strong desire to gain slave territory. They received this opportunity after the Gadsden Purchase, made with the purpose of building a transcontinental railroad through the southern U.S. Knowing that Southerners would prefer more slave soil, Stephen Douglas compromised through the Kansas-Nebraska Act which allowed the Nebraska territory to be divided in half with the likelihood that Kansas would become a slave state so that he (Douglas) could have the railroad go through the North/Illinois. This led to a statewide civil war in Kansas known as Bleeding Kansas; while it is an essential component of the nation's path towards the Civil War, it would not have occurred if the South hadn't been desperate for more slave states...which only occurred because the territory from the Mexican Cession voted for free soil. As a result, it is more appropriate to view the Mexican War as the event when the Civil War originated.

Exercise 15: Short Answer Practice Question 4

Source Material

— Grant E. Hamilton, *The Sacrilegious Candidate*, 1896

SAQ 4 Prompt

Use the image above and your knowledge of U.S. history to answer parts (a), (b), and (c).

   (a) Explain the point of view reflected in the image.

   (b) Explain how one element of the image expresses the point of view identified in **(a)**.

   (c) Explain how the issue shown in the cartoon helped to shape one specific U.S. government action between 1900-1917.

Write a Response to SAQ 4

Sample Response to SAQ 4

Note: After completing your answer, we recommended you scratch out the letters (a), (b), and (c).

(a) The point of view shown in the cartoon is supportive of the wealthy capitalists and bankers that held the vast majority of power during the Gilded Age. They believed that William Jennings Bryan and his populist agenda will bring ruin to the United States. There is fear that using free and unlimited coinage of silver will destroy the American economy by creating an inflationary monetary policy that will undermine the financial security of the entire country while claiming that it is beneficial to help the indebted farmers. (b) The Bible laying on the ground is a key element in the imagery of this cartoon. The Bible is being trampled on while Bryan is clinging to the cross and the crown of thorns. Additionally, the pages of paper that Bryan is carrying have been ripped out of the Bible. The purpose of this imagery is to discredit Bryan as a religious man who supports the teachings of the Bible and instead show him as someone who will use religion for his own goals while not respecting the sanctity of religion. (c) The conflict between the lower and upper classes during the Gilded Age was addressed through legislation during the Reform Era. The populists led by Bryan had several other demands other than an inflationary monetary policy. They also wanted a graduated income tax which became law with the passage of the 16th Amendment. For Bryan and other populists, the value in this amendment was that it created an expectation that those with the most money would contribute the most in taxes while those with lower incomes or debt would contribute less, as they had little money they could afford to pay in taxes.

Chapter 6
All About Long Essay Questions
(LEQs)

Anatomy of an LEQ

The Long Essay Question (LEQ) section of the APUSH exam requires you to select and respond to **one of three questions** from **three different historical periods** that share the **same theme.** One of the historical period options will include recent historical events (up to the present day). Choose the one question you feel you can answer the best and disregard the other two.

The total amount of time for answering the Long Essay Question is **40 minutes.**

Understanding the LEQ Rubric

While the SAQ rubric is simply concerned with how fully and accurately you answered the questions asked, the LEQ rubric is more nuanced. When evaluating your response to the Long Essay Question, the reader is looking for you to demonstrate specific historical writing skills.

You can earn up to six points for your LEQ response. Points are awarded based on whether and how effectively you address the academic writing requirements outlined in the table that follows.

LEQ Writing Element Max. Possible Points	Requirement to Earn Points
Contextualization 1 Point	Response describes the broader historical context relevant to the prompt
Thesis 1 Point	Response addresses the prompt with a historically defensible claim that establishes a line of reasoning
Evidence 2 Points	Response supplies specific examples of evidence related to the prompt (1 point) OR Response goes beyond merely **identifying specific evidence** relevant to the prompt by **using that evidence to support an argument** related to the prompt (2 points)
Analysis and Reasoning 2 Points	Response uses historical reasoning to establish an argument that addresses the prompt. This can be done by applying any <u>one</u> of the following historical concepts: **Comparison, causation,** or **continuity and change over time.** (1 point) OR Response demonstrates a **complex understanding** of the topic by **using evidence to corroborate or qualify an argument** that addresses the prompt. This can be done by using any <u>one</u> of the following approaches: • Analyze the nuance of an issue by incorporating **multiple viewpoints**, explaining **similarities and differences**, explaining **continuity and change over time**, explaining **multiple causes**, or explaining **causes and effects** • Explain relevant and insightful **connections within and across periods** • Corroborate (reinforce the validity of) an argument by incorporating **multiple perspectives across themes** • Qualify (modify) an argument by considering **diverse or alternative viewpoints or evidence.** (2 points)

Tips for Tackling LEQs

Tip 1: Contextualization Belongs in Your Introduction

A point is given for providing contextualization. This skill requires you to give background information on the period of the essay question. There are two straightforward methods to earn this point. One method is to explain the events that led up to the years covered in the prompt. This provides background information. The second method is to explain the broad characteristics of the period that is covered in the question. Your introduction – including contextualization – should be approximately five to seven sentences. This ensures it will not be too short, which could reduce your chance of earning a point. If it is too long, you may not finish the entire essay.

Tip 2: Include a Strong Thesis Statement

Write your thesis statement at the end of your introduction; it should respond directly to the prompt. If time allows, you should include a refined version of your thesis in your conclusion. Your thesis statement needs to add new insight/new information. The readers of AP exam essay responses will not reward you with a point for merely rewording the question.

Tip 3: Use Strong Topic Sentences

Topic sentences should be claims that **support your thesis or main argument;** they should not be simple statements of fact. We include examples of what this looks like in the sample LEQ responses later in this chapter (starting on page 80).

There can be more than three topic sentences in your essay. A common strategy is to use the familiar five-paragraph structure for the LEQ:

1. Introduction / Thesis Statement
2. Evidence 1
3. Evidence 2
4. Evidence 3
5. Conclusion

This approach is acceptable; however, **do not feel limited to five paragraphs.** Good topic sentences can be a key component to earning points for the skill of **analysis.** The more strong topic sentences you include, the better chance your analysis is strong. Every time you address a new topic (country, region, president, policy, etc.), you should write a new topic sentence.

Tip 4: Use Historical Terms

Whenever possible, **use historical terms to demonstrate your knowledge.** For example, it is better to write the term "headright system" than to simply state that 50 acres of land was given to anyone who paid the passage for an indentured servant. This will help you gain points for the **evidence** component of the LEQ.

Tip 5: Organize Your Ideas

Present your ideas in an order that will help you clearly define **cause-and-effect relationships,** make **comparisons,** and address nuances of an issue by **analyzing multiple variables** in a logical manner. This will help you earn points with **analysis**.

Example of a Disorganized Response

Teddy Roosevelt passed two laws, the Pure Food and Drug Act and the Meat Inspection Act. This occurred because muckraker Upton Sinclair exposed the horrible conditions that existed in the meat-packing industry. Sinclair was part of a group of writers in the early 1900s that began to expose societal problems that had been hidden during the Gilded Age. After the public became outraged from reading Sinclair's book, *The Jungle*, Roosevelt passed these laws. Both of these laws were created to help protect the American consumer.

Example of an Organized Response

During the early 1900s, writers known as muckrakers began to expose societal problems that had been hidden during the Gilded Age. One of the muckrakers, Upton Sinclair, exposed the horrible conditions that existed in the meat-packing industry by writing about them in his fictional book *The Jungle*. The public was outraged that food was prepared in such unsanitary conditions, and as a result, President Teddy Roosevelt passed the Meat Inspection Act to help protect American consumers. Shortly thereafter, President Roosevelt expanded government regulation to protect consumers by passing the Pure Food and Drug Act.

Tip 6: Round Out Your Analysis

Many of the methods by which you can earn points for analysis have already been addressed. Here are a few additional tips to help you more fully develop your arguments and ideas and round out your analysis. Additionally, by incorporating the ideas listed you will include the historical thinking skills that are required in the essays in a manner that is natural within your writing.

- **Context:** Give accurate **background information** to help explain how additional forces influenced an event or to illustrate why an event was significant.

- **Causation:** When describing a **cause-and-effect relationship**, explain both the cause and effect in a manner that illustrates how the two points are related.

- **Continuity** and **Change:** If you are identifying the continuation of a trend, include evidence from an earlier period as well as the period you are writing about to show **similarities** between the two periods. If there is change, identify a **turning point**: develop an explanation of how things were, how the turning point was impactful, and how things changed following the event.

- **Comparison:** Identify two or more events, individuals, or historical eras and explain their **similarities or differences** using as many examples to provide evidence as possible.

When using **multiple variables** to explain an issue, each variable should be identified with its own topic sentence, and the rest of the paragraph should support that topic sentence. Then a new topic sentence can be constructed to address the next variable.

Tip 7: Get Two Opportunities to Earn the Complexity Point

- **A point is given for expressing historical complexity.** This skill requires you to connect information from the years provided in the question to a topic outside of the years provided. The most straightforward strategy for earning this point is to explain how the ideas in your essay connect with another event or period that occurs beyond the dates noted in the question.
- **A point is also given for analyzing nuance within your essay.** This can be achieved by writing a strong two-sentence thesis that includes multiple aspects of that help you respond to the prompt. You will need to support the multiple aspects throughout your essay to earn the point.

While you can only earn one complexity point, by following these two pieces of advice, you have two opportunities to earn the point. If one attempt is unsuccessful, the other attempt may not be.

Practice Responding to Long Essay Questions

This section provides sample essay prompts and responses to help you understand the best way to structure your own answers. Note how each response applies the techniques recommended in the *Tips for Tackling LEQs* section (see page 77).

Exercise 16: Long Essay Practice Question 1

LEQ 1 Prompt

Compare the Chesapeake and New England colonies from 1607-1692.

Write a Response to LEQ 1

_____

_____

_____

_____

_____

_____

_____

_____

_____

_____

_____

_____

_____

_____

_____

_____

The Spanish had begun to colonize the Americas in 1492 when Columbus arrived in Hispaniola. For the next century, other European nations had limited ability to colonize in the "New World." This allowed Spain to grow rich from the mineral wealth and cash crops of Latin America. However, when the Spanish armada was defeated by the English navy, other European nations began to colonize in the Americas. The English colonies developed much differently from the way the Spanish colonies did; in fact, the English colonies varied greatly among themselves. The Chesapeake colonies were created for financial profit; as a result, the primary focus was the economy, whereas the settlers who came to New England were intent on creating religious communities. It may appear that Maryland was similar to New England since it was created as a safe haven for Catholics; however, the development of the colony was much different than in New England as Maryland became tolerant of all Christian religions while Massachusetts Bay was intolerant of any who challenged the power of the Protestant Church.

The younger sons of wealthy Englishmen invested in colonies in the hopes of earning large profits. Due to primogeniture, only the eldest son inherited the father's property. As a result, the other sons wanted to find a method of increasing their wealth. After the failure of the lost colony of Roanoke, these sons began pooling their money through joint stock companies. The most famous of these companies, the Virginia Company, settled Jamestown. Initially, the men who arrived at Jamestown sought to profit by finding gold. However, it was John Rolfe's discovery that the soil was perfect for the cultivation of tobacco that led to the acquisition of profits.

Landowners needed a large workforce to maximize the profits they could make through cash crops. They were able to acquire these workers due to the enclosure system. Because England had made previously public lands private, the poor needed to gain access to land, and America was that opportunity. Since the poor did not have the money necessary to pay for the passage to America, they sold themselves into indentured servitude, believing that after fulfilling their seven-year obligation, they would be able to acquire land of their own. The process of indentured servitude created a compliant workforce until the headright system pushed freed indentured servants further west, making them vulnerable to Indian attacks. When they asked for help from the colony's governor, William Berkeley, to protect them, no assistance was given. This led to the outbreak of Bacon's Rebellion which, although unsuccessful, led the wealthy elite to become concerned about future uprisings. As a result, the labor force shifted to the use of African slaves.

In New England, the Massachusetts Bay Colony was created for religious reasons; the settlers sought to create a perfect Christian community. Those who settled in Massachusetts Bay were called Puritans and wanted to purify the Church of England rather than separate from it. Their governor, Jonathan Winthrop, proclaimed that the colony would be "a city upon a hill" which could serve as a model for all other religious communities. To achieve this vision, those who were viewed as obstacles were eliminated. Roger Williams was the first dissenter to challenge the power of the church by stating there should be a strict separation between church and state. As punishment for his statements, he was exiled and eventually set up the colony of Rhode Island. A second dissenter, Anne Hutchinson, began to teach a philosophy called antinomianism. She claimed that anyone who had been predestined did not have to follow the laws of God nor man. This statement undermined not only the power of the government but more importantly the power of church leaders, and she too was exiled.

Although Maryland, a Chesapeake colony, was created for religious reasons, its treatment of those with various religious beliefs was much more tolerant than in New England. Maryland was created by Lord Baltimore as a safe haven for Catholics. Over time, Protestants moved into Maryland in numbers large enough to create concern that they might overthrow the government and persecute the Catholics. As a result, the Acts of Toleration were created, which allowed for all Christians to worship freely, thereby allowing for a greater freedom of religion than was allowed in New England.

The differences in the ways of life in the various colonies continued beyond the colonial era. Following the American Revolution, several compromises needed to be made during the Constitutional Convention to ensure enough states would ratify the new government. Additionally, the differences between the regions would lead to conflicts over the sectional balance and ultimately become so divisive that compromise could no longer keep the nation united: Southern states seceded, and the Union and the Confederacy fought the Civil War.

Exercise 17: Long Essay Practice Question 2

LEQ 2 Prompt

To what extent was the Era of Good Feelings a period of harmony within the United States? Confine your answer to the years 1816-1833.

Write a Response to LEQ 2

_____

_____

_____

_____

_____

_____

_____

_____

_____

_____

_____

_____

_____

_____

_____

_____

_____

_____

_____

Sample Response to LEQ 2

During the War of 1812, the federal government imposed an embargo on trade with Britain. This hindrance to trade impacted the profits of New England businessmen. Frustrated over the situation, a group of Federalists met at the Hartford Convention and created a list of demands along with an ultimatum that if their demands were not met they would agitate for New England states to secede from the Union. However, by the time the Federalists' messengers arrived at the capitol, the war had ended. The Federalists were viewed as disloyal and their party disintegrated. With only the Democratic-Republican party intact, many Americans felt that the bitter partisanship that had existed would no longer be a part of American politics. Initially, the Era of Good Feelings was a period with a strong feeling of national pride; however, concern over representation in the Senate began to divide the nation along sectional lines. The Market Revolution exacerbated the divide between North and South, and the debate over federal and state power continued during this period. As a result, rather than a harmonious period, this was a tumultuous time in American history.

Before the War of 1812 ended, New England merchants (Federalists) met at the Hartford Convention to draft a list of demands which they thought would protect their economic interests in the future. However, when the demands were delivered, the war had already concluded through the signing of the Treaty of Ghent. In addition, there was a strong sense of nationalism due to Andrew Jackson's victory at the Battle of New Orleans. The demands led the Federalists in New England to appear disloyal. As a result, the Federalist party was diminished, most notably by the fact that no one ever ran for president as a Federalist again. This led to a view that with only one political party, political divisions would disappear; that was not the case.

Concerns about political representation in the Senate led to sectional divisions. Missouri was ready to become a state and the desire was for it to be a slave state. However, Northerners opposed this because it would give Southern/slave states more representation in the Senate. To resolve the issue, Henry Clay created the Missouri Compromise which kept the sectional balance by adding Missouri as a slave state and Maine as a free state. Although this created a peaceful resolution to the Missouri issue, it still highlighted that each section of the nation was concerned with political power and that there would be future conflict when the sectional balance was threatened.

In addition to political concerns, economic concerns also divided the nation along sectional lines. While it is true that the nation became more closely linked through improved infrastructure, this connection was not powerful enough to overcome the economic issues that arose. The Tariff of 1816 protected Northern industry, but it came at a cost to Southern farmers who were forced to pay for higher-priced goods. Issues continued to grow when the Panic of 1819 struck. Farmers had overspeculated on their loans from the Bank of the United States. As a result, their farms were foreclosed, and they blamed the federal government and the Eastern elites running the banks for their misfortune.

In 1828, Andrew Jackson won the presidential election and escalated the division between the states and the federal government. Before leaving the presidency, Adams signed the Tariff of 1828, which dramatically increased the tax on foreign goods. This had a positive impact on New England, but it was extremely costly to Southerners, who referred to the tax as the Tariff of Abominations. The state that challenged this tariff the most was South Carolina. They were led by the vice president, John C. Calhoun, who anonymously wrote the South Carolina Exposition advocating for nullification. The South Carolina legislature voted to nullify the tariff and thus began the Nullification Crisis. While Jackson did not care for the tariff, he would not allow the power of the presidency to be challenged. As a result, he prepared the military to attack South Carolina. However, before fighting began, Henry Clay was able to create the Compromise Tariff of 1833, lowering the tariff to a level Southerners would accept, while still protecting Northern manufacturing. To ensure he had the final word, Jackson passed the Force Bill, which stated that if any state refused to enforce a tariff, the military would force the state to comply, illustrating that there was still tension between the federal and state government.

The tension between federal and state government was also present in the courts. Cases were heard by the Marshall Court which asked the Supreme Court to determine whether state governments had overstepped their authority. One case, McCulloch v. Maryland, focused on the Bank of the United States. The state of Maryland desired to eliminate a branch of the bank within their borders and began to tax the bank. The Supreme Court heard the case and referred to the necessary and proper clause which determined the bank was constitutional. Since it was constitutional for the federal government to create the bank, it was determined it was unconstitutional for a state to destroy it. This reasserted federal power over the decision of a state. The case of Gibbons v. Ogden continued this trend when the Supreme Court determined it unconstitutional for a monopoly to be granted by the state of New York to a steamboat company that traveled between New York and New Jersey. The decision hinged on the Court's interpretation of "interstate commerce" (granted to the federal government through the Commerce Clause of the Constitution), which was determined to include navigation.

The conflicts over the sectional balance and economic policies during the Era of Good Feelings divided the nation along sectional lines. This division continued in the aftermath of the Mexican War. The additional territory that had been gained through the Mexican Cession led to further conflict between Northern and Southern states over federal representation. New compromises like the Kansas-Nebraska Act were initially viewed as a method to reduce this tension while providing economic opportunity to Northern states. However, instead of reducing tension, it only increased hostility between the free soil and pro-slavery factions in the United States.

Exercise 18: Long Essay Practice Question 3

LEQ 3 Prompt

Analyze the effects of the political and economic corruption during the Gilded Age, between 1865 and 1900.

Write a Response to LEQ 3

_____

_____

_____

_____

_____

_____

_____

_____

_____

_____

_____

_____

_____

_____

_____

_____

_____

_____

_____

_____

_____

_____

_____

_____

_____

_____

_____

_____

_____

_____

_____

_____

_____

_____

_____

_____

_____

_____

_____

_____

_____

_____

_____

_____

_____

Sample Response to LEQ 3

  The Gilded Age was an era in which the American government used a laissez-faire approach to governing. This allowed robber barons to use their wealth and influence to gain immense political and economic power, creating a massive income gap between the wealthy and the poor. Although there was a movement by some philanthropists to improve society, it was primarily to support public institutions, not to help the working class survive. This created an environment that embraced the concept of social Darwinism. During the Gilded Age, political machines forged alliances between politicians and business owners to maximize the wealth and power of the business elite. The government did little to regulate the power of big business. This allowed railroad owners to exploit small business owners and farmers, and the lack of government oversight allowed industrial trusts to perpetuate poor working conditions and unfair pricing practices.

  Political machines organized voting blocs to gain the loyalty of politicians who were then beholden to the needs of the business owners who had paid tribute to the political machine. Political machines were successful at organizing groups, specifically desperate immigrants, to vote for certain politicians. Once the machine ensured a candidate won the election, his loyalty was virtually assured. Businesses paid political machines to pressure these politicians to support their interests rather than the interests of the American people. As a result, little regulation occurred, and businesses were able to act without any method of counterbalancing their power.

  Owners of railroads used this lack of oversight to exploit Western farmers. During the Gilded Age, railroads were pressured by large trusts to offer rebates and kickbacks in order to secure large shipping contracts from the trusts. Due to this price competition, railroad companies became less profitable. In order to recover some of the revenue lost to these discounts, the railroads overcharged small

Western farmers to ship their goods. In cases where the railroads were concerned that a price war would hurt their business, the companies formed alliances known as pools, which served to share their business and their profits. Pools split the shipments from Western farmers across multiple railroads at fixed prices so that the farmers could not turn one railroad company against the other to try to get a lower shipping price for their crops. These practices by the railroads put Western farmers in a vulnerable position. They were not able to refuse payment to the railroads because any delay in shipping could lead to the spoiling of their crops.

Large-scale business was also making it difficult for small farmers to remain in business for themselves. Barbed-wire trusts and grain elevator trusts were overcharging small Western farmers. The farmers tried to resist by creating farmers' cooperatives as a method to produce their own products and services and avoid being overcharged by the trusts. The Grangers movement tried combine the resources of smaller farmers to organize their own supplies/silos. Unfortunately, this was not very successful. They also tried to form a political bloc to influence lawmakers. They almost had success with the passage of the Interstate Commerce Act, meant to ensure fair railroad practices. To enforce this new law, the Interstate Commerce Commission (ICC) was created; however, the railroad companies challenged the decisions of the ICC in the courts where corrupt judges were able to limit the effectiveness of the agency.

Wealthy donors also ensured that the president would support their interests. In 1896, the Populist Party supported candidate William Jennings Bryan, who demanded government take control of the railroads, create a graduated income tax and, most significantly, implement free and unlimited coinage of silver. Banks and wealthy creditors were against this policy and donated generously to opponent William McKinley's campaign, knowing that he opposed the coinage of silver and the creation of inflation. This support helped ensure that

McKinley won the 1896 election.

The federal government, influenced by machines and business leaders, carried out policies that protected the interests of businesses. In 1877, railroad workers' wages, already low, were cut by 10%, so the workers began to strike in several cities throughout the United States. However, the strike was ended when President Hayes sent troops to use force to end the strikes. The workers of the Pullman Palace Cars, led by Eugene Debs, also went on strike. Much like the strike in 1877, it was broken when railroad owners appealed to President Grover Cleveland to send in troops to ensure that there would be no interference with trains carrying the federal mail. Although these strikes were the first in a long line of strikes, they did set a precedent; because the government supported business, strikes were unsuccessful.

While the Gilded Age was an era dominated by political machines, powerful businessmen, and corrupt officials, the Progressive Era began to put power back into the hands of elected officials. Numerous reforms were enacted, specifically anti-trust legislation that broke up monopolies and allowed government to effectively regulate big business. As a result, workers and consumers benefited from the new government regulations that were implemented to help protect the safety and health of the American people.

Exercise 19: Long Essay Practice Question 4

LEQ 4 Prompt

To what extent were U.S. foreign policies successful from 1945 to 1964?

Write a Response to LEQ 4

_____

_____

_____

_____

_____

_____

_____

_____

_____

_____

_____

_____

_____

_____

_____

_____

_____

_____

_____

During World War II, the United States and Russia were allies, fighting with Britain against the Axis Powers. Near the end of the war, Franklin Roosevelt, Winston Churchill, and Joseph Stalin met at the Yalta Conference to discuss ways to avoid future issues between their nations. Despite these efforts, after World War II the United States and the Soviet Union were deeply suspicious of each other. This suspicion and the competition that followed led to the Cold War. For more than four decades, the two superpowers never fought against each other directly; however, they were involved in conflicts throughout the rest of the world in a battle for influence and supremacy. Immediately following WWII, the United States was successful at containing communism; however, during the 1950s and 1960s, the goal of rolling back communism was not accomplished; rather, communist governments spread to Latin America and Asia. Still, while the U.S. was drawn into the Vietnam War, it was able to avoid a large-scale nuclear war with the Soviet Union. As a result, this period was an era of mixed success in American foreign policy.

To stop communism from spreading, President Truman successfully adopted George Kennan's practice of containment. Containment included the Truman Doctrine which offered military support for the democratic government in Greece. Greece was involved in a civil war in which communist forces tried take control of the government. The Truman Doctrine also helped the Turks, who were being pressured by the Soviet Union to share control of a shipping route. Through U.S. support, the Turkish government retained control over the waterway. Additionally, the United States, through the Marshall Plan, gave billions of dollars to help non-communist nations rebuild their infrastructure. The belief was that if the democratic nations of Europe had help rebuilding, the democratic governments would be safe from the threat of communism.

President Truman was also successful at preventing Berlin from becoming wholly influenced by the Soviet Union. Berlin, one of the most important cities in Germany, had been divided by the U.S. and the Soviet Union; however, the entire city of Berlin was located in East Germany so the Soviet government began the Berlin Blockade. To overcome the blockade, President Truman instituted the Berlin Airlift. After nearly a year, the Soviets ended the blockade. This stopped the expansion of communism in Europe. It was also a victory for the U.S. in regard to its relationship with many nations in Europe. It proved that the United States would support European nations that were threatened by the Soviet Union.

Although the United States had great success in limiting the spread of communism in Europe, success in Asia was mixed. General MacArthur had successfully rebuilt Japan into a democratic nation. However, with the conclusion of WWII, the civil war in China reignited and Mao Zedong was able to lead the communist forces to victory. This made the most populous nation on the earth communist.

The Korean War threatened to continue the spread of communism in Asia. After WWII, Korea had been split at the 38th parallel. North Korea had become communist and South Korea was democratic. However, in 1950 the North Koreans sent tanks over the 38th parallel with the intention of reuniting the country under communist rule. Truman realized that the U.S. would have to assist the South Koreans if the country was going to avoid falling to communism. General MacArthur led U.S. troops and pushed the North Koreans back across the 38th parallel. MacArthur continued to push the North Korean military north, driving them back to the Yalu River. This threatened the Chinese (also communist), and the Chinese army began to assist the North Koreans which forced American troops to retreat behind the 38th parallel. This conflict was eventually resolved during President Dwight Eisenhower's administration when an armistice was declared and Korea remained permanently divided at the 38th parallel, containing the spread of communism.

It appeared that through NATO, Western Europe was secure against the spread of communism; however, there was a concern of communism spreading throughout Southeast Asia. This began when Vietnam wanted its independence from France. However, the French government was unwilling to give up its colony, and a war broke out. President Truman had the United States give the French financial support to fight the war. As a result, Ho Chi Minh looked to communist nations to support his war effort. A fear arose that if one nation in Southeast Asia fell to communism many others would follow, resulting in a large bloc of communist countries in Asia; this fear became known as the domino theory. France eventually gave up the war after losing a major battle at Dien Bien Phu, and Vietnam was split at the 17th parallel.

Shortly after his election, Kennedy unsuccessfully tried to reduce communist influence in the Western Hemisphere by supporting the Bay of Pigs Invasion in the hopes of overthrowing Fidel Castro. Castro had led a communist revolution in Cuba. This concerned American officials, who feared that a communist nation just 90 miles from the coast of Florida posed a threat to the United States. As a result, the CIA trained and armed Cuban exiles hoping that they could lead a successful counterrevolution. This operation was a complete failure which embarrassed Kennedy and created problems with Cuba in the near future.

   While U.S. foreign policy may have been successful during this period, challenges would continue for the U.S. government. The United States would become more involved in the conflict in Vietnam, costing tens of thousands of lives as the U.S. military escalated its presence in the southeast Asian nation. President Richard Nixon did successfully reduce tensions with China and the Soviet Union through détente; despite this, the U.S. military remained in Vietnam. The U.S. government would face further challenges in Iran when the U.S. embassy was overrun and Americans inside of the embassy were held hostage during the Iran Hostage Crisis. Nonetheless, the U.S. withstood these challenges and continued to support democratic governments and oppose communism. Eventually, the Soviet Union collapsed, bringing an end to the Cold War.

Chapter 7
All About Document-Based Questions (DBQs)

Anatomy of a DBQ

The Document-Based Question (DBQ) section of the test asks **one question** that requires you to take up to **eight sources (documents)** and synthesize them into a **unified response** that accurately addresses the question being asked. You will need to combine your analysis of the documents with information you have learned in class and from your text.

- The DBQ section begins with **15 minutes to read, analyze, and organize** the documents.

- You then have **45 minutes to write your response.**

The Document-Based Question has many similarities to the LEQ (although a DBQ will rarely ask you to examine events more recent than 1980). Pay close attention to the differences when approaching DBQs because addressing them is key to earning a high score.

Understanding the DBQ Rubric

The DBQ rubric is similar to that of the LEQ, but it is even more complex. When evaluating your response to the Document-Based Question, the reader is looking for you to demonstrate specific historical writing skills that focus on your analysis of primary and secondary sources.

You can earn up to seven points for your DBQ response. Points are awarded based on whether and how effectively you address the academic writing requirements outlined in the table that follows.

DBQ Writing Element Max. Possible Points	Requirement to Earn Points
Contextualization 1 Point	Response describes the broader historical context relevant to the prompt
Thesis 1 Point	Response addresses the prompt with a historically defensible claim that establishes a line of reasoning
Evidence From the Documents 2 Points	Addresses the prompt with content from <u>at least three</u> documents; **describes the documents** rather than simply quotes them (1 point) OR Response addresses the prompt using <u>at least six</u> documents as **evidence to support an argument**; goes beyond merely quoting the documents by **describing the documents** cited (2 points)
Evidence Beyond the Documents 1 Point	Response supplies at least one additional piece of historical evidence, outside of what is found in the documents, to help support the argument made in the thesis
Sourcing 1 Point	For <u>at least three</u> documents, response analyzes how or why each document's **historical situation, audience, point of view,** or **purpose** is relevant to the argument. You may apply a different analysis approach to each document chosen (e.g., you can describe the purpose of Doc. 1 and the historical situation of Doc. 2).
Complexity 1 Point	Response demonstrates a **complex understanding** of the topic by **using evidence to corroborate or qualify an argument** that addresses the prompt. This can be done by using any <u>one</u> of the following approaches: • Analyze the nuance of an issue by addressing **multiple viewpoints**, explaining the **similarities and differences**, explaining **continuity and change over time**, explaining **multiple causes**, or explaining **causes and effects** • Explain relevant and insightful **connections within and across historical periods** • Corroborate (reinforce the validity of) an argument by incorporating **multiple perspectives across themes** • Qualify (modify) an argument by incorporating **diverse or alternative viewpoints or evidence**.

Tips for Tackling DBQs

Tip 1: Use Contextualization in the Introductory Paragraph

A point is given for providing contextualization. This skill requires you to give background information on the time period covered in the essay prompt. There are two straightforward methods to earning this point. One method is to explain the events that came before the years covered in the prompt. This provides context (background information). The second method is to explain the broad characteristics of the period covered in the question. The contextualization should be approximately five to seven sentences. This ensures it will not be too short, which could reduce your chance of earning a point. If it is too long, you may not have time to address all of the elements that will improve your score, and you may not finish your essay.

Tip 2: Write a Clear Thesis Statement (No Introduction Required)

DBQs are long and include a great deal of detail. In order to answer them completely, you will need approximately three to five sentences for your thesis statement.

- **The thesis statement will immediately follow your introduction/contextualization.**

- Ensure your thesis statement **addresses all parts of the question** so that you can earn all possible points.

Tip 3: Use Strong Topic Sentences

Because the DBQ is complex, it is very likely that the traditional five-paragraph structure will be inadequate to fully answer the question. As a result, do not feel that you are constrained to five paragraphs. But **for each paragraph you do write, make sure to include a clear topic sentence.**

See *Tip 3: Use Strong Topic Sentences* in the LEQ chapter (page 77) for more advice.

Tip 4: Use Historical Terms

As with the LEQ, you should **showcase your knowledge of relevant historical terms** when answering the DBQ.

See *Tip 4: Use Historical Terms* in the LEQ chapter (page 78) for additional tips.

Tip 5: Organize Your Ideas and Highlight Relationships Using Transition Phrases

A good DBQ response requires the coherent, well-organized presentation of arguments and evidence addressing multiple source documents. As such, it is critical that you **organize your ideas.** Make it easy for the reader to follow your answer by **grouping related ideas** and presenting ideas in a **logical sequence** to support the conclusion you are trying to argue.

Use verbal cues to show the relationship between ideas. Start sentences with **transition phrases** like the following, to signal where you are going with your next statement:

- Similarly, ...
- By contrast, ...
- However, ...
- As a result, ...
- For example, ...
- Additionally, ...

For more ideas, see *Tip 5: Organize Your Ideas* in the LEQ chapter (page 78).

Tip 6: Write and Annotate a Detailed Analysis

In addition to the information given in *Tip 6: Round Out Your Analysis* in the LEQ chapter (page 79), you must incorporate the following elements to score well on a DBQ response:

- **Accurately describe the content of a minimum of three documents.** To complete this step, you must accurately summarize the information in the document. Treat the document like a piece of evidence or example you learned in class. Incorporate the information in the document in a manner that helps support your topic sentence and your overarching argument (thesis statement). This should be done by including statistics and ideas provided in the document. It should also include your analysis of those statistics and ideas. By completing the steps above, you may earn one point. If you do not analyze at least three documents, you will not receive any points for this requirement.

- **Avoid using quotes.** You do not need quotes to earn points for using the documents. Additionally, students frequently misuse quotes and do not earn the points for using documents. If you feel you must include the use of quotes, keep them short! It is essential to show your understanding of the material. This can be done by using a short quote and explaining the quote through the use of academic verbs (e.g., this quote *illustrates, demonstrates, illuminates, highlights,* or *implies*).

- **Bonus point: Accurately incorporate the content of at least six documents to support an argument in response to the prompt.** This will allow you to earn two points rather than the single point you would earn for analyzing just 3-5 documents.

- **Cite each document in parentheses,** in the following manner: **(Doc. ___).** You should not use a full citation such as the title of the document; rather, just indicate which document you used for your information by placing the corresponding number after the abbreviation "Doc." (e.g., Doc. 1, Doc. 2). For example:

  > *Although Lincoln was focused on Western lands, Southern states felt his election was a threat to all slave owners. As a result, South Carolina seceded from the Union after Lincoln's election, pointing out that Northern states were not following the Fugitive Slave Act and were acting outside of the Constitution. South Carolina dissolved its bond with the Union and declared that it was a nation unto itself (Doc. 4).*

- **Use stems to help focus in on the key information for the sourcing point.** Describe how or why the document's historical situation, audience, purpose, or point of view is relevant to the argument presented in your thesis statement or topic sentence. You should use a combination of these stems a total of three times in your essay.

Historical Situation	During this time... During this era... At the time the document was written...
Audience	The author was targeting _____ because... The author was addressing _____ because... This was meant for _____ because...
Purpose	The author's intention was _____ because... The author wrote this because... The author hoped to _____ because... By repeatedly referring to (or referencing, or commenting upon) _____, the speaker/writer is trying to...
Point of View	Because the speaker/writer had a stake in... Because the speaker's success (or profitability, or influence) was contingent on... The credibility of the speaker is questionable (or indisputable) because...

- **Use outside information to support your thesis.** You must include information and concepts learned from class or your textbook to bolster your argument. This information should be introduced in a similar manner to your response to the Long Essay Question, where you will be using information you learned from class lecture or readings. This point is one of the easiest to earn. Ensure that you take the time in include one piece of outside information to increase your chances of earning the highest score you possibly can.

Tip 7: Give Yourself Two Opportunities to Earn the Complexity Point

There are multiple approaches for earning the complexity point; however, few students are able to successfully earn this point. You can improve your chances of earning this elusive point by using two methods that will strengthen your writing and should be manageable in a timed situation.

- The complexity point can be earned by connecting information from the years provided in the question to a topic outside of the years provided. The most straightforward strategy for earning this point is to **explain how the ideas in your essay connect with another event or period that occurs beyond the dates listed**. This is done by providing and introduction/contextualization from before the date in the prompt and by discussing future historical events in the conclusion. Both the introduction and the conclusion must be on the same topic that is referenced in the prompt.

- A point can also be earned for **analyzing nuance** within your essay. This can be achieved by writing a strong two-sentence thesis that includes multiple aspects of that help you respond to the prompt. You will need to support the multiple aspects throughout your essay to earn the point.

While you can only earn one complexity point, by following these two pieces of advice, you have two opportunities to earn the point. If one attempt is unsuccessful, the other attempt may not be.

Practice DBQs, One Document at a Time

The answers to DBQs require a complex set of skills. To make this more manageable, this section will help you practice each skill individually:

1. **Examine the document** to gain a quick understanding of what is being presented.

2. **Break down the document systematically,** using the checklist we provide for each document type.

3. **Read our sample analytical summary** of the document to understand how to express the most important information about the document in a concise manner. (Later in this chapter, you will practice writing your own analytical summaries.)

4. **Repeat** steps 1-3 for each document.

After you have practiced analyzing the documents one at a time, we will help you put the individual skills together to create a dynamic, complex, and comprehensive response to the DBQ (see the exercises starting on page 143).

The DBQ requires the analysis of multiple documents to support your thesis throughout your body paragraphs. Study the samples and then complete the practice exercises to hone your skills.

Exercise 20: Single-Document Analysis 1

Document 1: Map

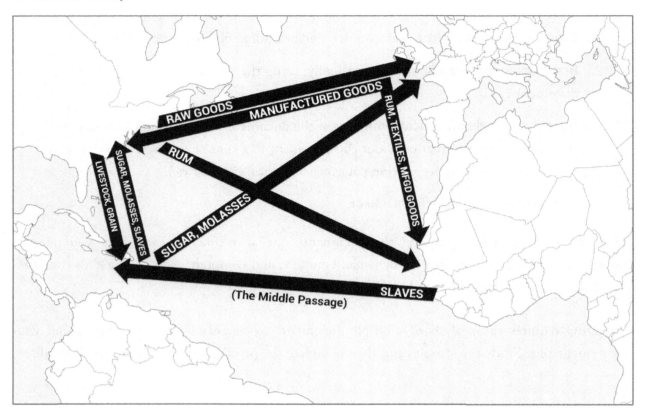

— *Transatlantic Trade Routes During the Colonial Era*

Analyze the Map

Directions: Fill out the grid below to identify the most important aspects of the map. Being able to describe the information depicted in the map will be critical in your DBQ response.

MEET THE MAP.	
Type *(check all that apply)* ☐ Political ☐ Exploration ☐ Census ☐ Survey ☐ Transportation ☐ Population/Settlement ☐ Land Use ☐ Planning ☐ Physical	
What is the title?	
What is the legend?	
OBSERVE ITS PARTS.	
What place or places are shown?	
What is labeled?	
If there are symbols, what do they stand for?	
When is it from?	
TRY TO MAKE SENSE OF IT.	
What was happening at the time this map was made? *(Historical Situation)*	
Why was it created? List evidence from the map that leads to your conclusion. *(Purpose)*	
Write one sentence summarizing the map.	

USE IT AS HISTORICAL EVIDENCE.	
What did you find out from this map that you might not learn anywhere else?	
What other documents or historical evidence are you going to use to help you understand this event or topic?	

Sample Analytical Summary of the Map

The British wanted to maximize their profitability from the American colonies. During this era, the British believed in the economic philosophy of mercantilism, which supported the belief that colonies existed for the enrichment of the "mother country." As a result, transatlantic trade routes were established in which the colonists could trade with Great Britain or its colonies in Africa or the Caribbean. To ensure the colonists traded exclusively with Britain and not with its European rivals, the Navigation Acts were created. This allowed the British to obtain low-cost materials which they could make into manufactured goods in their factories. Once the manufacturing process was complete, the colonists were expected to buy manufactured goods only from the British. However, the colonists did not like these restrictive practices and found other trade routes that would allow them to profit. One of these routes was the triangle trade. A map of this route illustrates that colonists from New England would travel to West Africa where they would trade rum for Africans whom they forced into slavery. The enslaved people were then transported through the Middle Passage to the West Indies. There, the New England shippers would trade them for molasses (often this trade was done with the French in violation of the Navigation Acts). Most of them would be forced to work on plantations in Brazil or the West Indies. In the final leg of the triangle trade, the shippers would bring the molasses back to New England where it would be used in the production of rum.

Exercise 21: Single-Document Analysis 2

Document 2: Diagram

THEORETICAL TOWNSHIP DIAGRAM
SHOWING
METHOD OF NUMBERING SECTIONS
WITH ADJOINING SECTIONS

36	31	32	33	34	35	36	31
80 Ch.	— — — — — 6 Miles — 480 Chains — — — — —						80 Ch.
1	6 (1 Mile)	5	4	3	2	1 (80 Ch.)	6
12	7	8	9	10	11	12	7
13	18	17	16	15	14	13	18
24	19	20	21	22	23	24	19
25	30	29	28	27	26	25	30
36	31	32	33	34	35	36	31
1	6	5	4	3	2	1	6

6 Miles — 480 Chains

T.T.S.

2

— *General Land Office Plan for Numbering Sections of a Standard Survey Township, 1796*

Analyze the Diagram

Directions: Fill out the grid below to identify the most important aspects of the diagram. Being able to describe the information in the diagram will be critical in your DBQ response.

MEET THE DIAGRAM.	
Type (*check all that apply*) ☐ Political ☐ Exploration ☐ Census ☐ Survey ☐ Transportation ☐ Population/Settlement ☐ Land Use ☐ Planning ☐ Physical	
What is the title?	
What is the legend?	
OBSERVE ITS PARTS.	
What facts or information are shown?	
What is labeled?	
If there are symbols, what do they stand for?	
When is it from?	
TRY TO MAKE SENSE OF IT.	
What was happening at the time this diagram was made? (*Historical Situation*)	
Why was it created? List evidence from the diagram that leads to your conclusion. (*Purpose*)	
Write one sentence summarizing the diagram.	

USE IT AS HISTORICAL EVIDENCE.	
What did you find out from this diagram that you might not learn anywhere else?	
What other documents or historical evidence are you going to use to help you understand this event or topic?	

Sample Analytical Summary of the Diagram

Under the Articles of Confederation, the Land Ordinance created an orderly way for the government to divide and sell land that was gained in the Old Northwest. To illustrate this division, sketches were created to create an orderly division of land that would be divided into towns, each town would be comprised of 36 sections, 1 mile by 1 mile each, which could be subdivided if necessary. Americans would have the ability to buy sections of this land to develop. However, one of the 36 sections, located near the center, had to be reserved for a school to be built upon as a way to encourage public education. Inhabiting this land was initially very challenging. The British were arming Indian tribes in the region who frequently attacked settlers who desired to take the land the Indians had lived on for generations.

Exercise 22: Single-Document Analysis 3

Document 3: Data Table

State	Pop. White	% White	Pop. Black	% Black	Population with ⅗ Compromise
Pennsylvania*	319,950	97.5%	7,855	2.5%	324,663
New York	189,647	90.0%	21,054	10.0%	202,279
New Hampshire	87,261	99.5%	541	0.5%	87,261
Virginia*	317,422	59.0%	220,582	41.0%	449,771
South Carolina	83,000	46.0%	97,000	54.0%	141,200
Georgia	35,240	63.0%	20,831	37.0%	47,738

— *Projected Population by Race,* 1780

*Most populated states in the North and the South (respectively)

Analyze the Data Table

Directions: Fill out the grid below to identify the most important aspects of the data table. Being able to describe the information expressed in the data will be critical in your DBQ response.

MEET THE DOCUMENT.	
Type *(check all that apply)*	
☐ Letter ☐ Report ☐ Newspaper	
☐ Advertisement ☐ Memorandum ☐ Congressional document	
☐ Chart or Table ☐ Speech ☐ Other	
☐ Court document ☐ Presidential document _____	
OBSERVE ITS PARTS.	
Who created it?	
Who read/received it? *(Audience)*	
When is it from? *(Historical Situation)*	
Where is it from? *(Historical Situation)*	
TRY TO MAKE SENSE OF IT.	
What is it talking about?	
Write one sentence summarizing the document.	
Why was it created? *(Purpose or Point of View)*	
Quote evidence from the document that illustrates your statement above.	
What was happening at the time in history this table covers? *(Historical Situation)*	

USE IT AS HISTORICAL EVIDENCE.	
What did you find out from this document that you might not learn anywhere else?	
What other documents or historical evidence are you going to use to help you understand this topic?	

Sample Analytical Summary of the Data Table

When the Constitutional Convention began in 1787, two plans were proposed for the formation of a legislature. The New Jersey Plan supported small states through the creation of a unicameral legislature and allowed each state an equal number of representatives. A different plan, the Virginia Plan, was created with the desire of giving more power to the larger states through the creation of a bicameral legislature in which representation in both houses would be determined by population. During this time, the Northern states had a significantly smaller population of enslaved people than the South due to the rocky soil and the harsh winters that did not accommodate plantation agriculture. The Southern state of Virginia was the largest state in the country, outnumbering the next closest state (Pennsylvania) by almost 200,000 people (if enslaved people were to be counted in a state's population). To resolve the conflict between the large and small states, the Great Compromise was created, which allowed for a bicameral legislature in which the number of representatives in the lower house was determined by population and the upper house was apportioned equally (two representatives per state). However, concerns about representation continued. Southern states wanted enslaved people to be counted in their population. By including enslaved people, the population of the Southern states would have increased dramatically. To solve the dispute over how to count the population, the Three-Fifths Compromise was created, which allowed each slave to be counted as three-fifths of a person. This kept parity between the population of the North and the South and allowed for the eventual ratification of the Constitution.

Exercise 23: Single-Document Analysis 4

Document 4: Speech

"Gentlemen, I have had men watching you for a long time and I am convinced that you have used the funds of the bank to speculate in the breadstuffs of the country. When you won, you divided the profits amongst you, and when you lost, you charged it to the bank. You tell me that if I take the deposits from the bank and annul its charter, I shall ruin ten thousand families. That may be true, gentlemen, but that is your sin! Should I let you go on, you will ruin fifty thousand families, and that would be my sin! You are a den of vipers and thieves."

— Andrew Jackson, 1836

Analyze the Speech

Directions: Fill out the grid below to identify the most important aspects of the speech. Being able to describe the information expressed in the speech is critical to your DBQ response.

MEET THE DOCUMENT.		
Type *(check all that apply)*		
☐ Letter	☐ Report	☐ Newspaper
☐ Advertisement	☐ Memorandum	☐ Congressional document
☐ Chart or Table	☐ Speech	☐ Other
☐ Court document	☐ Presidential document	_____

OBSERVE ITS PARTS.	
Who delivered it?	
Who read/received it? *(Audience)*	
When is it from? *(Historical Situation)*	
Where is it from? *(Historical Situation)*	

TRY TO MAKE SENSE OF IT.	
What is it talking about?	
Write one sentence summarizing the speech.	
Why was it written? *(Purpose or Point of View)*	
Quote evidence from the speech that illustrates your statement above.	
What was happening at the time in history this speech was written? *(Historical Situation)*	

USE IT AS HISTORICAL EVIDENCE.	
What did you find out from this speech that you might not learn anywhere else?	
What other documents or historical evidence are you going to use to help you understand this topic?	

Sample Analytical Summary of the Speech

Henry Clay attempted to become president in 1832 by setting up Andrew Jackson to veto the recharter of the Bank of the United States. Clay believed that the American people would be outraged by the veto and that Jackson would be defeated in the upcoming election. Jackson was not going to be intimidated by Clay's actions. Rather, because Jackson's blamed the Bank of the United States for the panic of 1819 and his political success was contingent on maintaining the support of "the common man," he attacked Clay and others who supported the bank as opportunists who used the bank's profits to increase their own wealth. Jackson continued to attack the bank's supporters by expressing that by eliminating the bank, many more families would be protected rather than harmed. This statement demonstrates Jackson's justifications for prematurely removing the money in the Bank of the United States and his veto as a way to protect a large body of American citizens. Jackson adeptly created a position that would help him escape blame for any financial difficulties that might occur as a result of closing the bank. Because of this, he argued, it was his moral responsibility to protect the American people from the poisonous and deadly policies he alleged were supported by the "den of vipers and thieves" (otherwise known as politicians) who came before him.

Exercise 24: Single-Document Analysis 5

Document 5: Political Cartoon / Drawing

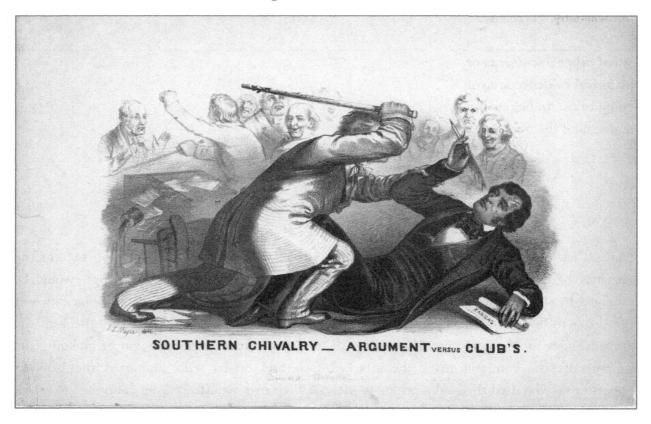

— John L. Magee, *Southern Chivalry – Argument versus Club's* (sic), 1856

Analyze the Political Cartoon

Directions: Fill out the grid below to identify the most important aspects of the cartoon. Being able to describe the information depicted in the drawing is critical to your DBQ response.

MEET THE CARTOON.	
Quickly scan the cartoon. What do you notice first?	
What is the title or caption?	
OBSERVE ITS PARTS.	
Words: Are there labels, descriptions, thoughts, or dialogue?	
Visuals: List the people, objects, and places in the cartoon.	
Visuals: List the actions or activities being shown in the illustration.	
TRY TO MAKE SENSE OF IT.	
Words: Which words or phrases are the most significant?	
Words: What adjectives describe the emotions portrayed?	
Visuals: Which of the visuals are symbolic?	
Visuals: What do the symbols stand for?	

Who drew this cartoon/drawing?	
When is it from?	
What was happening at the time in history it was created? *(Historical Situation)*	
What is the message? List evidence from the cartoon that led you to your conclusion. *(Purpose or Point of View)*	
USE IT AS HISTORICAL EVIDENCE.	
What did you find out from this image that you might not learn anywhere else?	
What other documents or historical evidence are you going to use to help you understand this event or topic?	

Sample Analytical Summary of the Cartoon

One cause of the Civil War was that politicians were unable to find methods of compromise to resolve sectional tension. This was illustrated when Congressman Preston Brooks from South Carolina beat Massachusetts Senator Charles Sumner in the Senate chambers with a cane. This was in retaliation for a speech Sumner gave called *The Crimes Against Kansas,* which insulted Senator Butler of South Carolina. A drawing of the incident accurately portrays other Southern politicians holding back senators who may have come to the aid of Sumner as he was beaten nearly to death. Additionally, the image shows that many Southern politicians supported this violent act. Not only did the event show political discourse breaking down between politicians, it also sought to intensify the divisions in the country by mocking Southerners' chivalry and insinuating to a targeted audience of free-soil supporters and abolitionists that Southerners were brutes who could not use more civilized forms of communication. In addition, the drawing implies that the fight between savagery and civilization is not over; rather, that the Northern cause will emerge victorious through the imagery of the pen being mightier than the sword (club).

Exercise 25: Single-Document Analysis 6

Document 6: Photograph

—Jacob Riis, *Shelter for immigrants in a Bayard Street tenement,* 1888.

Analyze the Photograph

Directions: Fill out the grid below to identify the most important aspects of the photograph.

Being able to describe the concepts depicted in the photo will be critical in your DBQ response.

MEET THE PHOTO.	
Quickly scan the photo. What do you notice first?	
Type *(check all that apply)* ☐ Portrait ☐ Landscape ☐ Posed ☐ Event ☐ Family ☐ Candid ☐ Documentary ☐ Action ☐ Architectural	
What is the title or caption?	
OBSERVE ITS PARTS.	
List the people you see.	
List the objects you see.	
List the activities you see.	
Write one sentence summarizing this photo.	
TRY TO MAKE SENSE OF IT (ANSWER TO THE BEST OF YOUR ABILITY; CAPTIONS MAY HELP).	
Who took the photo?	
Where is it from?	
When is it from?	
What is happening at the time in history this photo was taken? *(Historical Situation)*	

Why was it taken? List evidence from the photo that led you to this conclusion. *(Purpose or Point of View)*	
USE IT AS HISTORICAL EVIDENCE.	
What did you find out from this photo that you might not learn anywhere else?	
What other documents or historical evidence are you going to use to help you understand this event or topic?	

Sample Analytical Summary of the Photograph

Photographs captured by Jacob Riis during the Progressive Era were meant to illuminate the desperate living conditions of the poor. In the book he published, *How the Other Half Lives,* Riis included photos depicting poverty in the slums of cities. At this time, local governments embraced laissez faire policies that emboldened slumlords – property owners who desired to maximize their profits to rent out small spaces, designed for high occupancy, in tenement apartments to impoverished people. These buildings were so overcrowded it created a breeding ground for disease. Additionally, due to the poor ventilation, lung diseases like bronchitis were widespread. Overcrowded tenements also created a major threat in the event of a fire. They were constructed of wood, and because they were overfilled, it would be difficult for the large numbers of inhabitants to escape should a fire break out.

Exercise 26: Single-Document Analysis 7

Document 7: Political Cartoon

— Leonard Raven-Hill, *The Gap in the Bridge*, 1919

Analyze the Political Cartoon

Directions: Fill out the grid below to identify the most important aspects of the cartoon.
Being able to describe the information depicted in the drawing is critical to your DBQ response.

MEET THE CARTOON.	
Quickly scan the cartoon. What do you notice first?	
What is the title or caption?	
OBSERVE ITS PARTS.	
Words: Are there labels, descriptions, thoughts, or dialogue?	
Visuals: List the people, objects, and places in the cartoon.	
Visuals: List the actions or activities being shown in the illustration.	
TRY TO MAKE SENSE OF IT.	
Words: Which words or phrases are the most significant?	
Words: What adjectives describe the emotions portrayed?	
Visuals: Which of the visuals are symbolic?	
Visuals: What do the symbols stand for?	

Who drew this cartoon/drawing?	
When is it from?	
What was happening at the time in history it was created? *(Historical Situation)*	
What is the message? List evidence from the cartoon that led you to your conclusion. *(Purpose or Point of View)*	
USE IT AS HISTORICAL EVIDENCE.	
What did you find out from this image that you might not learn anywhere else?	
What other documents or historical evidence are you going to use to help you understand this event or topic?	

Sample Analytical Summary of the Cartoon

After WWI ended, Woodrow Wilson advocated strongly for the creation of the League of Nations, an organization he believed would be able to prevent future conflicts from occurring. Wilson was able to get acceptance of the League by European countries like Belgium, France, England, and Italy. However, astute political commentators at the time highlighted the major failure in the League was that the United States was not a member. Henry Cabot Lodge had led a group of Republican senators to oppose the League, and as a result, the most important nation for ensuring the League's success, the United States, was left out of this organization. Because the cartoonist was interested in influencing public opinion, he provided his candid assessment that although the League existed without the United States, the organization was not constructed as it was designed. He believed that because the United States was relaxing rather than taking on its essential role in maintaining global peace and stability, a gap has been exposed which would lead ultimately to failure.

Exercise 27: Single-Document Analysis 8

Document 8: Data Table

Before 1934	1959	1970	1975	2000
50%	35%	25%	15%	10%

— Percentage of Elderly Americans Living in Poverty by Year

Analyze the Data Table

Directions: Fill out the grid below to identify the most important aspects of the data table. Being able to describe the information expressed in the data will be critical in your DBQ response.

MEET THE DOCUMENT.		
Type *(check all that apply)*		
☐ Letter	☐ Report	☐ Newspaper
☐ Advertisement	☐ Memorandum	☐ Congressional document
☐ Chart or Table	☐ Speech	☐ Other
☐ Court document	☐ Presidential document	_____

OBSERVE ITS PARTS.	
Who created it?	
Who read/received it? *(Audience)*	
When is it from? *(Historical Situation)*	
Where is it from? *(Historical Situation)*	

TRY TO MAKE SENSE OF IT.	
What is it talking about?	
Write one sentence summarizing the document.	
Why was it created? *(Purpose or Point of View)*	
Quote evidence from the document that illustrates your statement above.	
What was happening at the time in history this table covers? *(Historical Situation)*	

USE IT AS HISTORICAL EVIDENCE.	
What did you find out from this document that you might not learn anywhere else?	
What other documents or historical evidence are you going to use to help you understand this topic?	

Sample Analytical Summary of the Data Table

Before 1934 half of the elderly population in America was living in poverty. However, this number was reduced through the passage of the Social Security Act, which was part of Franklin Roosevelt's New Deal. These statistics illustrate that the percentage of the elderly population living in poverty decreased from 50% before 1934 to 35% in 1959, demonstrating that this act was a success. This success was partly because the government started allocating money for the formerly employed to live on, but also because amendments were made so that the survivors (wife/children) of former workers could continue to receive benefits after the worker passed away, and because the amount of the Social Security benefits increased. The elderly population continued to benefit from improvements in Social Security when, in 1950, a decision was made to include a cost-of-living adjustment which increased the value of the payments to match inflation. During the 1960s, the age of recipients dropped from 65 to 62, giving elderly people who were desperate for assistance help earlier. However, the most significant change was the creation of Medicare in 1965, which offered government-subsidized healthcare for the elderly. This greatly reduced medical costs and helped reduce the number of elderly people in poverty to 25% in 1970 and to 15% in 1975. By repeatedly measuring (referencing) the number of elderly Americans living in poverty, the analysis in this data table is attempting to measure the level of success government programs had in reducing poverty among this group. The data suggestions the program created by Roosevelt initially helped many Americans; however, it was adjustments made by the Social Security Administration and future presidents that led to the dramatic lowering of the poverty rate among the elderly in the United States.

Practice Writing Comprehensive DBQ Responses

To give you practice in writing a comprehensive DBQ response, you will build upon the analytical skills you practiced in Exercises 20-27 (starting on page 118). For each document provided in the exercises in this section, you will:

1. **Examine the document** to gain a quick understanding of what is being presented.

2. **Break down the document systematically,** using the checklist we provide for each document type.

3. **Write an analytical summary** of the document that captures the most important information about the document in a concise manner.

4. **Repeat** steps 1-3 for each document.

5. **Write a comprehensive response** that incorporates your analysis of 5 or more documents.

6. **Read our sample comprehensive response** to see an example of a well-structured, thorough response.

7. **Compare our comprehensive response to yours.** Look at the similarities and differences. Focusing on the differences can help you identify alternative approaches to presenting your analysis in a more effective way.

Exercise 28: Comprehensive DBQ Analysis 1

Document 1: Pamphlet

"As to government matters, it is not in the power of Britain to do this continent justice: The business of it will soon be too weighty, and intricate, to be managed with any tolerable degree of convenience, by a power, so distant from us, and so very ignorant of us; for if they cannot conquer us, they cannot govern us...."

— Thomas Paine, *Common Sense*, 1775

Part 1: Analyze the Pamphlet

Directions: Fill out the grid below to identify the most important aspects of the pamphlet.
Being able to describe the information expressed in the pamphlet is critical to your DBQ response.

MEET THE DOCUMENT.		
Type *(check all that apply)*		
☐ Letter	☐ Report	☐ Newspaper
☐ Advertisement	☐ Memorandum	☐ Congressional document
☐ Chart or Table	☐ Speech	☐ Other
☐ Court document	☐ Presidential document	_____

OBSERVE ITS PARTS.	
Who wrote it?	
Who read/received it? *(Audience)*	
When is it from? *(Historical Situation)*	
Where is it from? *(Historical Situation)*	

TRY TO MAKE SENSE OF IT.	
What is it talking about?	
Write one sentence summarizing the document.	
Why was it written? *(Purpose or Point of View)*	
Quote evidence from the document that illustrates your statement above.	
What was happening at the time in history this document was written? *(Historical Situation)*	

USE IT AS HISTORICAL EVIDENCE.	
What did you find out from this document that you might not learn anywhere else?	
What other documents or historical evidence are you going to use to help you understand this event or topic?	

Part 2: Write an Analytical Summary of the Document

_____

_____

_____

_____

_____

_____

_____

_____

_____

Document 2: Map

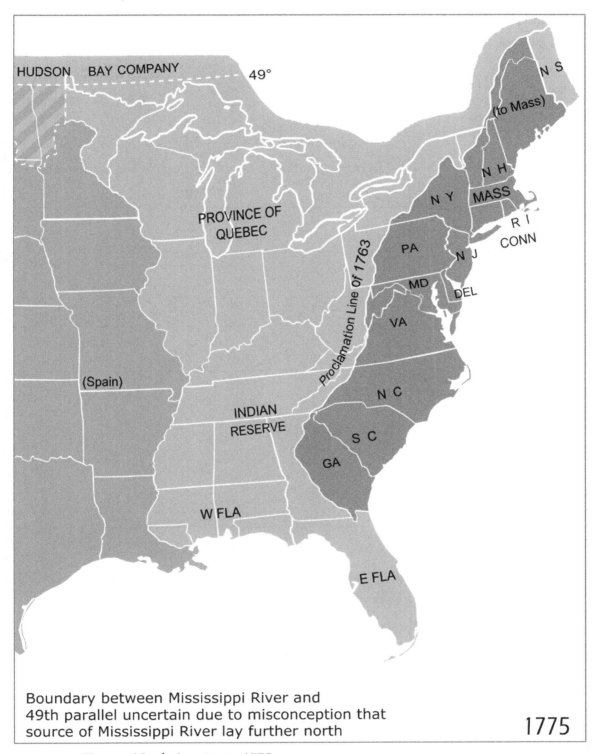

Boundary between Mississippi River and 49th parallel uncertain due to misconception that source of Mississippi River lay further north

1775

— *Eastern North America in 1775*

(Adapted from a scan from the *National Atlas of the United States*)

Directions: Fill out the grid below to identify the most important aspects of the map. Being able to describe the information depicted in the map will be critical in your DBQ response.

MEET THE MAP.	
Type *(check all that apply)* ☐ Political ☐ Exploration ☐ Census ☐ Survey ☐ Transportation ☐ Population/Settlement ☐ Land Use ☐ Planning ☐ Physical	
What is the title?	
What is the legend?	
OBSERVE ITS PARTS.	
What place or places are shown?	
What is labeled?	
If there are symbols, what do they stand for?	
When is it from?	
TRY TO MAKE SENSE OF IT.	
What was happening at the time this map was made? *(Historical Situation)*	
Why was it created? List evidence from the map that leads to your conclusion. *(Purpose)*	
Write one sentence summarizing the map.	

USE IT AS HISTORICAL EVIDENCE.	
What did you find out from this map that you might not learn anywhere else?	
What other documents or historical evidence are you going to use to help you understand this event or topic?	

Part 2: Write an Analytical Summary of the Document

_____

_____

_____

_____

_____

_____

_____

_____

_____

Document 3: Governmental Act

"WHEREAS it is expedient that a revenue should be raised in your Majesty's dominions in America, for making a more certain and adequate provision for defraying the charge of the administration of justice, and the support of civil government, ... we, your Majesty's most dutiful and loyal subjects...in parliament assembled, have therefore resolved to give and grant unto your Majesty the several rates and duties herein after mentioned..."

— Parliament of Great Britain, *The Townshend Act,* 1767

Part 1: Analyze the Document

Directions: Fill out the grid below to identify the most important aspects of the document.

Being able to describe the information expressed in the text is critical to your DBQ response.

MEET THE DOCUMENT.		
Type *(check all that apply)*		
☐ Letter	☐ Report	☐ Newspaper
☐ Advertisement	☐ Memorandum	☐ Congressional document
☐ Chart or Table	☐ Speech	☐ Other
☐ Court document	☐ Presidential document	_____

OBSERVE ITS PARTS.	
Who wrote it?	
Who read/received it? *(Audience)*	
When is it from? *(Historical Situation)*	
Where is it from? *(Historical Situation)*	

TRY TO MAKE SENSE OF IT.	
What is it talking about?	
Write one sentence summarizing the document.	
Why was it written? *(Purpose or Point of View)*	
Quote evidence from the document that illustrates your statement above.	
What was happening at the time in history this document was written? *(Historical Situation)*	

USE IT AS HISTORICAL EVIDENCE.	
What did you find out from this document that you might not learn anywhere else?	
What other documents or historical evidence are you going to use to help you understand this event or topic?	

Part 2: Write an Analytical Summary of the Document

_____

_____

_____

_____

_____

_____

_____

_____

_____

Document 4: Political Cartoon

— Philip Dawe, *The Bostonians Paying the Excise-man, or Tarring and Feathering*, 1774

Part 1: Analyze the Political Cartoon

Directions: Fill out the grid below to identify the most important aspects of the cartoon. Being able to describe the information depicted in the drawing is critical to your DBQ response.

MEET THE CARTOON.	
Quickly scan the cartoon. What do you notice first?	
What is the title or caption?	
OBSERVE ITS PARTS.	
Words: Are there labels, descriptions, thoughts, or dialogue?	
Visuals: List the people, objects, and places in the cartoon.	
Visuals: List the actions or activities being shown in the illustration.	
TRY TO MAKE SENSE OF IT.	
Words: Which words or phrases are the most significant?	
Words: What adjectives describe the emotions portrayed?	
Visuals: Which of the visuals are symbolic?	
Visuals: What do the symbols stand for?	
Who drew this cartoon/drawing?	

When is it from?	
What was happening at the time in history it was created? *(Historical Situation)*	
What is the message? List evidence from the cartoon that led you to your conclusion. *(Purpose or Point of View)*	
USE IT AS HISTORICAL EVIDENCE.	
What did you find out from this image that you might not learn anywhere else?	
What other documents or historical evidence are you going to use to help you understand this event or topic?	

Part 2: Write an Analytical Summary of the Document

_____

_____

_____

_____

_____

_____

_____

_____

_____

_____

Document 5: Governmental Act

"AN ACT FOR THE BETTER SECURING THE DEPENDENCY OF HIS MAJESTY'S DOMINIONS IN AMERICA UPON THE CROWN AND PARLIAMENT OF GREAT BRITAIN.

"That the said colonies ... in America have been, are, and of right ought to be, subordinate unto, and dependent upon the imperial crown and parliament of Great Britain; and that the King's majesty... had, hath, and of right ought to have, full power and authority to make laws and statutes of sufficient force and validity to bind the colonies and people of America, subjects of the crown of Great Britain, in all cases whatsoever,

"II. And be it further declared and enacted by the authority aforesaid, That all resolutions, votes, orders, and proceedings, in any of the said colonies ... whereby the power and authority of the parliament of Great Britain, to make laws and statutes ... is denied, or drawn into question, are, and are hereby declared to be, utterly null and void to all in purposes whatsoever."

— The Parliament of Great Britain, *Declaratory Act*, 1766

Part 1: Analyze the Document

Directions: Fill out the grid below to identify the most important aspects of the document.
Being able to describe the information expressed in the text is critical to your DBQ response.

MEET THE DOCUMENT.		
Type *(check all that apply)*		
☐ Letter	☐ Report	☐ Newspaper
☐ Advertisement	☐ Memorandum	☐ Congressional document
☐ Chart or Table	☐ Speech	☐ Other
☐ Court document	☐ Presidential document	_____

OBSERVE ITS PARTS.	
Who wrote it?	
Who read/received it? *(Audience)*	
When is it from? *(Historical Situation)*	
Where is it from? *(Historical Situation)*	

TRY TO MAKE SENSE OF IT.	
What is it talking about?	
Write one sentence summarizing the document.	
Why was it written? *(Purpose or Point of View)*	
Quote evidence from the document that illustrates your statement above.	
What was happening at the time in history this document was written? *(Historical Situation)*	

USE IT AS HISTORICAL EVIDENCE.	
What did you find out from this document that you might not learn anywhere else?	
What other documents or historical evidence are you going to use to help you understand this event or topic?	

Part 2: Write an Analytical Summary of the Document

_____

_____

_____

_____

_____

_____

_____

_____

Document 6: Governmental Legislation

"WHEREAS dangerous commotions and insurrections have been fomented and raised in the town of Boston...to the subversion of his Majesty's government, and to the utter destruction of the publick (sic) peace, and good order of the said town; in which commotions and insurrections certain valuable cargoes of teas, were seized and destroyed. [F]rom and after the first day of June, one thousand seven hundred and seventy-four, it shall not be lawful for any person or persons whatsoever to lade put off or from any quay, wharf, or other place, within the said town of Boston, or in or upon any part of the shore of the bay, commonly called The Harbour of Boston...."

— The Boston Port Act, 1774 (one of the Coercive Acts)

Part 1: Analyze the Text

Directions: Fill out the grid below to identify the most important aspects of the document.
Being able to describe the information expressed in the text is critical to your DBQ response.

MEET THE DOCUMENT.		
Type *(check all that apply)*		
☐ Letter	☐ Report	☐ Newspaper
☐ Advertisement	☐ Memorandum	☐ Congressional document
☐ Chart or Table	☐ Speech	☐ Other
☐ Court document	☐ Presidential document	_____

OBSERVE ITS PARTS.	
Who wrote it?	
Who read/received it? *(Audience)*	
When is it from? *(Historical Situation)*	
Where is it from? *(Historical Situation)*	

TRY TO MAKE SENSE OF IT.	
What is it talking about?	
Write one sentence summarizing the document.	
Why was it written? *(Purpose or Point of View)*	
Quote evidence from the document that illustrates your statement above.	
What was happening at the time in history this document was written? *(Historical Situation)*	

USE IT AS HISTORICAL EVIDENCE.	
What did you find out from this document that you might not learn anywhere else?	
What other documents or historical evidence are you going to use to help you understand this event or topic?	

Part 2: Write an Analytical Summary of the Document

_____

_____

_____

_____

_____

_____

_____

_____

_____

Tying It All Together: DBQ Practice Question 1

Now that you have analyzed each document individually, it is time to put all of the information together in an organized and coherent essay. To practice this, respond to the prompt below. Include the information you summarized while analyzing each of the documents provided earlier in this section, as well as outside information you have learned in class or from a text.

DBQ 1 Prompt

Explain the evolution of the American independence movement from 1763 through 1776. In your answer, analyze the role of economics, politics, and ideology; comment on how the British response to the colonists' concerns contributed to the growing conflict. Use at least six documents to support your analysis.

Write a Comprehensive DBQ Response

_____

_____

_____

_____

_____

_____

_____

_____

_____

_____

_____

_____

DBQ 1: Compare Your Response to a Sample Response

Compare your essay to the sample written below. Your essay does not need to be exactly the same to be written well. However, it should reflect several commonalities. If your essay seems similar in structure/organization, content/evidence, and analysis, you have answered the question well. If there are major differences in these areas, it would be beneficial to note what the differences are and determine if you your writing would be stronger by adopting a model that corresponds with the sample.

DBQ 1 Prompt

Explain the evolution of the American independence movement from 1763 through 1776. In your answer, analyze the role of economics, politics, and ideology; comment on how the British response to the colonists' concerns contributed to the growing conflict.

Sample Comprehensive DBQ Response

The colonists supported the British during the French and Indian War in the pursuit of more land which could provide them with new economic opportunities. George Washington had led a colonial militia into the Ohio River Valley with the intention of gaining settlements for the English colonists. However, French forces were successful at driving Washington and his men back to Virginia. In response, Britain sent segments of its military to help defeat the French and their Indian allies. The colonists were eager to assist the British; however, when they joined the British forces, they were treated as second-class soldiers. The colonists suffered these indignities due to their belief that when the war ended, a new tract of land, valuable for farming, would be made available to them. Following the French and Indian War, the colonists were optimistic that they would be able to benefit from their relationship with the British by expanding into the Ohio River Valley. However, the British government was focused on its own treasury and wanted to ensure the colonists allowed them to gain wealth rather than spend Great Britain's wealth on the protection and development of the colonies. As the British implemented policies that threatened the colonists' economic opportunities, disputes arose not only over economic policy but also over politics. When violence began to break out, the colonists became more committed to the beliefs of the radical Whigs and Enlightenment thinkers. As a result, they committed themselves to a new form of government based on republicanism which could be achieved only through a war to free themselves from the control of the British.

When the war ended, the colonists became frustrated at British policies that put the well-being of the British treasury before economic opportunities for the colonists. Following the war, Pontiac, a Huron chief who felt threatened by the encroachment of English settlers, initiated an uprising (Pontiac's Uprising) which was almost successful in defeating the British forces. The uprising was stopped only when the British tricked Pontiac by giving him blankets infected with smallpox. Once the Indians were defeated, the British forbade the colonists from crossing the Appalachian Mountains into land reserved for Indians through the Proclamation of 1763 (Doc. 2). This policy was to prevent future wars from occurring between the colonists and the Indians, and if these wars were prevented, the British would not have to spend the government's precious money on defending the colonies. While this policy angered the colonists, it should not have come as a surprise. The British, believing in the philosophy of mercantilism, felt the colonies should bring them wealth rather than cost them money to maintain.

The British continued to try to gain wealth from the colonists which led to the colonists believing that their rights as Englishmen were being abused. Following the French and Indian War, the British passed the Sugar Act. This tax was levied to recover the money the British had spent during the war. The colonists were displeased by this tax; however, they accepted it with little resistance since they believed the British had the right to place indirect taxes on goods. However, the British were not gaining enough money from this tax and so added a second tax, the Stamp Act. This tax enraged colonists because it was a direct tax. The colonists felt that the British did not have a right to place a direct tax on them unless they had representation in Parliament (which the colonists did not have). As a result, the colonists formed the Stamp Act Congress to document its list of grievances; it also instituted the nonimportation agreements, a boycott which was meant to hurt the British where it mattered most: economics. Colonial leaders maintained that the British had no right to place this tax on them and that the tax must be resisted. To help prevent the tax from being collected, Sam Adams organized the Sons of Liberty to punish and humiliate tax collectors by attacking them. Although the British did eventually remove the Stamp Act, they immediately passed the Declaratory Act which stated that the British government had the ability to pass any laws it desired. The British believed this act was necessary to better secure the colonies by clearly stating they were subordinate to the British crown. In addition to stating that the British had the right to pass any laws they desired, the Declaratory Act continued by stating that any laws that the colonies passed that violated British laws were "invalid." The Parliament hoped to create a legal justification for British control of the colonies if they should continue to challenge the authority of the British government (Doc. 5).

The colonists did not accept British authority; rather, they continued to protest with the intention that it would lead to the British giving them the rights of Englishmen as well as the natural rights they believed they were entitled to. Parliament had created another new tax, the Townshend Act, which placed a small tax on a number of imports. While this was an indirect tax, which the colonists had previously accepted, protests erupted. The colonists were angry that the tax gathered from the Townshend Act was going to be used to pay the governor's salary (Doc. 3). This was problematic because at the time the document was written, the governor's salary was managed by the colonial legislature. This was important because it created a check on the governor's power. If the governor ignored the legislature, it could punish him by lowering his salary. With this new tax/payment of the salary, the colonial legislature lost its power of the purse and the governor seemed to be wholly answerable to the King and the British parliament. In response, colonists in Boston began to protest, and this protest was met with a show of force by the British military. As tensions between the two groups heightened, the troops began to fire at the colonists, which led to the death of five colonial protesters. This event further seemed to prove to the colonists that the British troops who had been placed in the colonies and were living amongst them through the Quartering Act were not there to protect them, but rather to control them. Additionally, the colonists feared that not only were their rights as Englishmen being threatened but also their natural right to life as professed by John Locke.

Colonists began to question whether they could resolve their conflict with Britain, as the British government continued to create harsh punishments for colonial protests. When an additional tax was placed on tea, Sam Adams led the Sons of Liberty to participate in the Boston Tea Party. The British responded to this action by demonizing the colonists. A British political cartoon showed the colonists with sinister looks on their faces forcing tea down the throat of a tax collector. In addition to this insult, the colonists were shown to be injuring the tax collector by tarring and feathering him. The threat of further violence was also depicted by the noose hanging from the tree and in the background, the image showed colonists dumping tea into Boston Harbor to highlight their most recent affront against the British. Finally, a copy of the Stamp Act was shown posted on the tree as a reminder of the colonists' earlier opposition to the British through the Stamp Act Congress. Although this cartoon was a strong rebuke of the colonists' defiant actions, because the cartoonist was British his reliability of the events depicted is questionable, as his loyalties were to England (Doc. 4). The British government was enraged by all of these acts, especially the destruction of the tea, and in response, it passed the Coercive Acts, renamed the Intolerable Acts by the colonists. Parliament's intention was to punish the colonists because the government believed that the colonists could be intimidated into ending their insurrection against the British government. These acts restricted the colonists' rights as Englishmen as well as their natural rights. Specifically, the acts prevented the use of Boston Harbor until the tea that had been destroyed was paid for, which threatened the economic well-being of the merchants of Boston. Additionally, it removed the charter from Boston; this meant that the residents of the city were no longer guaranteed the rights of Englishmen. Finally, the Acts protected government officials who were involved in actions that led to the murder of colonists from being charged with murder, therefore violating right to life (Doc. 6).

The colonists finally began to feel they must become independent when violent confrontations could not be resolved through a peaceful process. The English military attempted to secure weapons held in colonial arsenals near Boston. While the British were able to secure the weapons at Lexington, the colonists defeated them at Concord. The next clash between the British and the colonists was at Bunker Hill. Although the British eventually took Bunker Hill, they faced a difficult battle and suffered many casualties. At the Second Continental Congress, the colonists drafted the Olive Branch Petition which offered their loyalty if the British would cease the attacks on the colonies. Instead the British declared the colonies to be in rebellion. In response, Thomas Paine wrote and published his pamphlet, Common Sense. Paine believed that although the colonists had tried to reconcile with the British government, the effort had been unsuccessful (and would continue to be unsuccessful) because Britain's government did not have the capacity to treat colonists living on the American continent with the respect that they deserved. Paine also asserted that the issues that emerged in America were too complex for Britain, so far away and ignorant of the challenges that colonists faced, that they could not effectively govern them. In fact, the only way the British could govern them (ineffectively) would be to conquer them, which would mean the colonists would no longer be Englishmen, but rather second-class subjects (Doc. 1). Therefore, Paine urged colonists to fight for their independence, which would lead to the creation of a republican form of government rather than submitting or attempting further reconciliation with the British government. Paine's call for independence was supported, and in 1776, the colonists declared their independence from the British.

Initially, the colonists had interacted with the British in a manner that indicated a desire to remain part of Great Britain. However, when issues transitioned from economic to political conflict, and when it appeared that the British could no longer govern America in a manner consistent with the ideological beliefs of the colonists, colonial leaders became successful in their call for a war for independence. This determination for autonomy from the British would exist beyond the revolution. During the Napoleonic Wars, the British began to attack American ships, restricting trade and impressing American sailors. This outraged the American government and after a series of unsuccessful economic responses, the United States once again waged war against the British during the War of 1812. Although in many ways the war was considered a draw, it did prove that Americans expected their national rights to be respected and were willing to fight to ensure they would be.

Exercise 29: Comprehensive DBQ Analysis 2

Document 1: Neutrality Proclamation

"Whereas it appears that a state of war exists between Austria, Prussia, Sardinia, Great-Britain, and the United Netherlands, of the one part, and France on the other, and the duty and interest of the United States require, that they should with sincerity and good faith adopt and pursue a conduct friendly and impartial toward the belligerent powers:

"...And I do hereby also make known that whosoever of the citizens of the United States shall render himself liable to punishment or forfeiture under the law of nations, by committing, aiding or abetting hostilities against any of the said powers, or by carrying to any of them those articles, which are deemed contraband by the *modern* usage of nations."

— George Washington, 1793

Part 1: Analyze the Document

Directions: Fill out the grid below to identify the most important aspects of the document.

Being able to describe the information in the document is critical to your DBQ response.

MEET THE DOCUMENT.		
Type *(check all that apply)*		
☐ Letter	☐ Report	☐ Newspaper
☐ Advertisement	☐ Memorandum	☐ Congressional document
☐ Chart or Table	☐ Speech	☐ Other
☐ Court document	☐ Presidential document	_____

OBSERVE ITS PARTS.	
Who wrote it?	
Who read/received it? *(Audience)*	
When is it from? *(Historical Situation)*	
Where is it from? *(Historical Situation)*	

TRY TO MAKE SENSE OF IT.	
What is it talking about?	
Write one sentence summarizing the document.	
Why was it written? *(Purpose or Point of View)*	
Quote evidence from the document that illustrates your statement above.	
What was happening at the time in history this document was written? *(Historical Situation)*	

USE IT AS HISTORICAL EVIDENCE.	
What did you find out from this document that you might not learn anywhere else?	
What other documents or historical evidence are you going to use to help you understand this event or topic?	

Part 2: Write an Analytical Summary of the Document

_____

_____

_____

_____

_____

_____

_____

_____

Document 2: Political Cartoon

— Alexander Anderson, *Ograbme, or the American Snapping Turtle,* 1807

Part 1: Analyze the Political Cartoon

Directions: Fill out the grid below to identify the most important aspects of the cartoon. Being able to describe the information depicted in the drawing is critical to your DBQ response.

MEET THE CARTOON.	
Quickly scan the cartoon. What do you notice first?	
What is the title or caption?	
OBSERVE ITS PARTS.	
Words: Are there labels, descriptions, thoughts, or dialogue?	
Visuals: List the people, objects, and places in the cartoon.	
Visuals: List the actions or activities being shown in the illustration.	
TRY TO MAKE SENSE OF IT.	
Words: Which words or phrases are the most significant?	
Words: What adjectives describe the emotions portrayed?	
Visuals: Which of the visuals are symbolic?	
Visuals: What do the symbols stand for?	
Who drew this cartoon/drawing?	

When is it from?	
What was happening at the time in history it was created? *(Historical Situation)*	
What is the message? List evidence from the cartoon that led you to your conclusion. *(Purpose or Point of View)*	
USE IT AS HISTORICAL EVIDENCE.	
What did you find out from this image that you might not learn anywhere else?	
What other documents or historical evidence are you going to use to help you understand this event or topic?	

Part 2: Write an Analytical Summary of the Document

_____

_____

_____

_____

_____

_____

_____

_____

_____

_____

Document 3: Convention of 1800

"Article 1:

There shall be a firm, inviolable, and universal peace, and a true and sincere Friendship between the French Republic, and the United States of America, and between their respective countries, territories, cities, towns, and people without exception of persons, or places.

"Article 2:

The Ministers...not being able to agree at present respecting the Treaty of Alliance...will negotiate further at a convenient time, [and] the Convention will have no operation, and the two nations will be regulated as follows...(the obligations of the two nations are listed in the remaining articles)."

— *Convention of 1800*

Part 1: Analyze the Text

Directions: Fill out the grid below to identify the most important aspects of the document.
Being able to describe the information in the document is critical to your DBQ response.

MEET THE DOCUMENT.		
Type *(check all that apply)*		
☐ Letter	☐ Report	☐ Newspaper
☐ Advertisement	☐ Memorandum	☐ Congressional document
☐ Chart or Table	☐ Speech	☐ Other
☐ Court document	☐ Presidential document	_____

OBSERVE ITS PARTS.	
Who wrote it?	
Who read/received it? *(Audience)*	
When is it from? *(Historical Situation)*	
Where is it from? *(Historical Situation)*	

TRY TO MAKE SENSE OF IT.	
What is it talking about?	
Write one sentence summarizing the document.	
Why was it written? *(Purpose or Point of View)*	
Quote evidence from the document that illustrates your statement above.	
What was happening at the time in history this document was written? *(Historical Situation)*	

USE IT AS HISTORICAL EVIDENCE.	
What did you find out from this document that you might not learn anywhere else?	
What other documents or historical evidence are you going to use to help you understand this event or topic?	

Part 2: Write an Analytical Summary of the Document

_____

_____

_____

_____

_____

_____

_____

_____

_____

Document 4: Political Cartoon

— Victor, *Keep Off: The Monroe Doctrine Must Be Respected*, 1823

Directions: Fill out the grid below to identify the most important aspects of the cartoon. Being able to describe the information depicted in the drawing is critical to your DBQ response.

MEET THE CARTOON.	
Quickly scan the cartoon. What do you notice first?	
What is the title or caption?	
OBSERVE ITS PARTS.	
Words: Are there labels, descriptions, thoughts, or dialogue?	
Visuals: List the people, objects, and places in the cartoon.	
Visuals: List the actions or activities being shown in the illustration.	
TRY TO MAKE SENSE OF IT.	
Words: Which words or phrases are the most significant?	
Words: What adjectives describe the emotions portrayed?	
Visuals: Which of the visuals are symbolic?	
Visuals: What do the symbols stand for?	
Who drew this cartoon/drawing?	

When is it from?	
What was happening at the time in history it was created? *(Historical Situation)*	
What is the message? List evidence from the cartoon that led you to your conclusion. *(Purpose or Point of View)*	
USE IT AS HISTORICAL EVIDENCE.	
What did you find out from this image that you might not learn anywhere else?	
What other documents or historical evidence are you going to use to help you understand this event or topic?	

Part 2: Write an Analytical Summary of the Document

_____

_____

_____

_____

_____

_____

_____

_____

_____

Document 5: Map

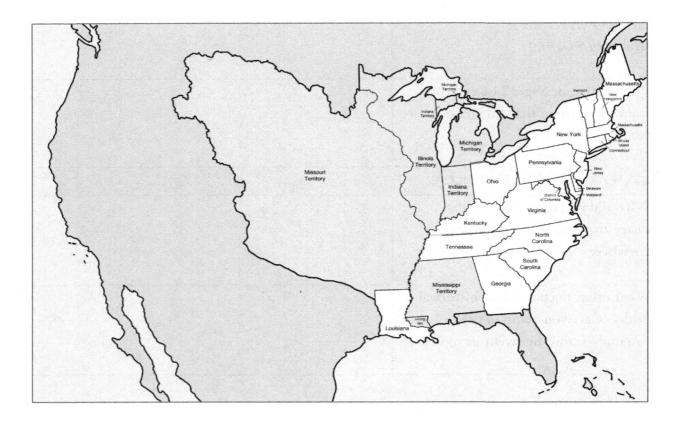

— *States and Territories of the United States of America, June 4, 1812 to August 4, 1812*

Part 1: Analyze the Map

Directions: Fill out the grid below to identify the most important aspects of the map. Being able to describe the information depicted in the map will be critical in your DBQ response.

MEET THE MAP.	
Type *(check all that apply)* ☐ Political ☐ Exploration ☐ Census ☐ Survey ☐ Transportation ☐ Population/Settlement ☐ Land Use ☐ Planning ☐ Physical	
What is the title?	
What is the legend?	
OBSERVE ITS PARTS.	
What place or places are shown?	
What is labeled?	
If there are symbols, what do they stand for?	
When is it from?	
TRY TO MAKE SENSE OF IT.	
What was happening at the time this map was made? *(Historical Situation)*	
Why was it created? List evidence from the map that leads to your conclusion. *(Purpose)*	
Write one sentence summarizing the map.	

USE IT AS HISTORICAL EVIDENCE.	
What did you find out from this map that you might not learn anywhere else?	
What other documents or historical evidence are you going to use to help you understand this event or topic?	

Part 2: Write an Analytical Summary of the Document

_____

_____

_____

_____

_____

_____

_____

_____

_____

_____

Document 6: Treaty

"ARTICLE II

His Catholic Majesty cedes to the United States...all the territories which belong to him, situated to the eastward of the Mississippi, known by the name of East and West Florida."

— Adams-Onis Treaty, 1819

Directions: Fill out the grid below to identify the most important aspects of the document. Being able to describe the information in the document is critical to your DBQ response.

MEET THE DOCUMENT.		
Type *(check all that apply)*		
☐ Letter	☐ Report	☐ Newspaper
☐ Advertisement	☐ Memorandum	☐ Congressional document
☐ Chart or Table	☐ Speech	☐ Other
☐ Court document	☐ Presidential document	_____

OBSERVE ITS PARTS.	
Who wrote it?	
Who read/received it? *(Audience)*	
When is it from? *(Historical Situation)*	
Where is it from? *(Historical Situation)*	

TRY TO MAKE SENSE OF IT.	
What is it talking about?	
Write one sentence summarizing the document.	
Why was it written? *(Purpose or Point of View)*	
Quote evidence from the document that illustrates your statement above.	
What was happening at the time in history this document was written? *(Historical Situation)*	

USE IT AS HISTORICAL EVIDENCE.	
What did you find out from this document that you might not learn anywhere else?	
What other documents or historical evidence are you going to use to help you understand this event or topic?	

Part 2: Write an Analytical Summary of the Document

_____

_____

_____

_____

_____

_____

_____

_____

_____

Document 7: Treaty

"The Pasha of Tripoli shall deliver up to the American Squadron now off Tripoli, all the Americans in his possession; and all the subjects of the Pasha of Tripoli now in the power of the United States of America shall be delivered up to him; and as the number of Americans in possession of the Pasha of Tripoli amounts to 300 persons, more or less; and the number of Tripolino subjects in the power of the Americans to about 100 more or less, the Pasha of Tripoli shall receive from the United States of America, the sum of $60,000 as a payment for the difference between the prisoners herein mentioned."

— Treaty Ending the Tripolitan War, 1805

Part 1: Analyze the Document

Directions: Fill out the grid below to identify the most important aspects of the document.
Being able to describe the information in the document is critical to your DBQ response.

MEET THE DOCUMENT.		
Type *(check all that apply)*		
☐ Letter	☐ Report	☐ Newspaper
☐ Advertisement	☐ Memorandum	☐ Congressional document
☐ Chart or Table	☐ Speech	☐ Other
☐ Court document	☐ Presidential document	_____

OBSERVE ITS PARTS.	
Who wrote it?	
Who read/received it? *(Audience)*	
When is it from? *(Historical Situation)*	
Where is it from? *(Historical Situation)*	

TRY TO MAKE SENSE OF IT.	
What is it talking about?	
Write one sentence summarizing the document.	
Why was it written? *(Purpose or Point of View)*	
Quote evidence from the document that illustrates your statement above.	
What was happening at the time in history this document was written? *(Historical Situation)*	

USE IT AS HISTORICAL EVIDENCE.	
What did you find out from this document that you might not learn anywhere else?	
What other documents or historical evidence are you going to use to help you understand this event or topic?	

Part 2: Write an Analytical Summary of the Document

_____

_____

_____

_____

_____

_____

_____

_____

_____

Tying It All Together: DBQ Practice Question 2

Now that you have analyzed each document individually, it is time to put all of the information together in an organized and coherent essay. To practice this, respond to the prompt below. Include the information you summarized while analyzing each of the documents provided earlier in this section, as well as outside information you have learned in class or from a text.

DBQ 2 Prompt

Evaluate to what extent American foreign policy remained consistent from the period of 1792 through 1824.

Write a Comprehensive DBQ Response

_____

_____

_____

_____

_____

_____

_____

_____

_____

_____

_____

_____

_____

DBQ 2: Compare Your Response to a Sample Response

Compare your essay to the sample written below. Your essay does not need to be exactly the same to be written well. However, it should reflect several commonalities. If your essay seems similar in structure/organization, content/evidence, and analysis, you have answered the question well. If there are major differences in these areas, it would be beneficial to note what the differences are and determine if you your writing would be stronger by adopting a model that corresponds with the sample.

DBQ 2 Prompt

Evaluate to what extent American foreign policy remained consistent from the period of 1792 through 1824.

Sample Comprehensive DBQ Response

George Washington followed a strict policy of isolation as president and attempted to ensure this isolationist policy would continue. During the Revolutionary War, France had signed the Franco-American Treaty which promised that both nations would assist each other in a time of war. This alliance was essential for the colonists' victory over the British. However, although the colonists had embraced foreign alliances during the American Revolution, the new nation's interactions with foreign nations shifted shortly after the conclusion of the American Revolution. After America won its independence, the country was weak and vulnerable to foreign interference. As a result, the initial impulse of the early presidents was to avoid alliances and foreign wars if at all possible. Still, America was drawn into foreign conflicts. What must be noted is that after any foreign conflicts ended, the U.S. avoided maintaining an international presence and instead returned to isolation. Additionally, efforts were made to ensure that European influence was removed from the North and South American continents, which helped to isolate the United States even further. As a result, there was absolute consistency in how American leaders carried out the nation's isolationist foreign policy.

Like Washington, President Adams attempted to avoid foreign conflicts, and while he was unable to avoid them, he was successful at making the U.S. more isolated following the conflict. American merchant ships, trading in the Caribbean, were being attacked by the British and French navies. The British attacks ended after the signing of Jay's Treaty, but the French, angry that the U.S. refused to continue to pay back its loan from the Revolutionary War, increased their attacks. Adams, hoping to avoid getting drawn into the war, sent three diplomats to France to negotiate with the foreign minister, Talleyrand. When the American diplomats arrived, they were told they would have to pay a bribe before meeting Talleyrand. The diplomats returned to America and angrily recounted their treatment in what became known as the XYZ Affair. Many Federalists (Adams' own party) desired war, but instead of declaring war, a quasi-war occurred in which American naval ships attacked French privateers. At the same time, the European War was proving difficult for the French, and Napoleon wanted to prevent the U.S. joining his adversaries. Additionally, if the U.S. was neutral, the British may have allowed it to trade with France, giving the French many of the supplies they so desperately needed. As a result, the U.S. and France agreed to the Convention of 1800, which ended the hostility as well as the alliance between the two countries (Doc. 3). This not only ended the alliance with the French, but also allowed the U.S. to isolate itself from European nations.

Like Adams, Jefferson was drawn into a foreign war and was able to return to isolation following an American victory. During this time, the Barbary pirates, who operated off the coast of North Africa, had forced the Washington and Adams administrations to pay them tribute in return for allowing American ships to pass through the Mediterranean Sea. This was an extremely costly policy; the tribute was one-fifth of the entire nation's budget. Jefferson refused to pay it, so the pirates began attacking American ships and holding the crews for ransom. In response, Jefferson increased the strength of the navy and began the Tripolitan War. After defeating the Barbary pirates, Jefferson agreed to peace with the Pasha of Tripoli through a prisoner exchange. Since the Americans had approximately 200 fewer prisoners, the U.S. also agreed to pay $60,000 as a payment for the difference (Doc. 7). This amount was significantly less than the ransom originally required. The victory and the resulting treaty demonstrated that the United States desired this matter to be over and for American ships to be able to travel throughout the Mediterranean Sea without being attacked.

As president, Jefferson successfully isolated the United States from France. Napoleon's wars in Europe had proved costly and the loss of Haiti meant that controlling the Port of New Orleans was no longer essential for the French. So, when Jefferson had diplomats offer to buy a small section of land that included the Port of New Orleans, Napoleon countered with an offer to sell the U.S. all of the Louisiana Territory. Although Jefferson knew that a deal like this required the consent of Congress, he agreed to Napoleon's terms, fearful that if he waited too long the opportunity for the U.S. to acquire the land might be lost. As a result, Jefferson applied loose construction, a philosophy he had previously argued against. Jefferson was willing to contradict his strict constructionist beliefs for two reasons: First, the map shows that the opportunity to gain this land was a great deal; it nearly doubled the size of the U.S. Second, it illustrates that the land being acquired would allow Jefferson to further isolate the United States by removing the French from North America (Doc. 5).

Conflicts between the British and the French continued to make it difficult for the U.S. to remain isolated. The British wanted to cut off America's trade with France and in 1807 passed the Orders in Council which declared that the U.S. could not trade with France unless it entered a British port first. The British set up a blockade which not only stopped American ships but also impressed American sailors. Jefferson was outraged but did not want to be drawn into the war, so the U.S. passed the Embargo Act which stated that American ships were not allowed to trade with foreign nations. This law hurt the American economy greatly. A political cartoon drawn at the time shows the embargo as a snapping turtle labelled "Ograbme" or "embargo" spelled backwards. The cartoonist shows that American merchants had quality (superfine) goods to sell, but they were unable to due to the embargo holding them back (Doc. 2). Because this was a political cartoon the artist was provided a one-sided assessment that he believed would resonate with the customers who bought the papers. The cartoonist was accurate, in that the embargo bred a great deal of resentment, and Jefferson realized this type of commercial isolation was ineffective and counterproductive. In response, Jefferson attempted to restrict trade to the British and the French only through the Non-Intercourse Acts. However, since Britain and France were two of the largest trading partners with the U.S., this also was ineffective. As a result, James Madison had to deal with the issue when he became president. To address this, he implemented Macon's Bill #2. The result of this bill was that the French promised to stop attacking American ships, but the British did not, so the U.S. declared war against Britain in the War of 1812.

When the War of 1812 was over, the U.S. began to implement policies that allowed its economy to operate with less reliance on the European market. During the war, American factories had begun to produce more goods and sell them domestically. When the Treaty of Ghent ended the war, the American government wanted to protect the American factories so the first protective tariff, the Tariff of 1816, was passed. This was the start of Henry Clay's American System. While the high tariffs protected American factories, a strong national banking system permitted business loans to be given from American banks and American businesses to expand. Improved and expanded infrastructure enabled each section of the country to specialize in one economic area. This allowed raw materials to be moved within the country and finished goods to be sold throughout the nation. This national economy helped limit the U.S.'s reliance on foreign nations.

Monroe was able to continue Jefferson's policy of isolation by removing the Spanish from the southeastern border of the United States. During this time, Andrew Jackson, involved in fighting wars against the Indians, ignored orders. Jackson was in pursuit of the Seminoles when they crossed into Spanish Florida. Jackson pursued them across the border and attacked Spanish forts. The Spanish government realized they would struggle to hold the territory and, as a result, agreed to the Adams-Onis Treaty which ceded all Spanish territories "situated eastward of the Mississippi" to the United States (Doc. 6). In return, the U.S. promised it would not contest Spain's possessions west of the Mississippi River.

The United States government was able to isolate the nation further still when revolutions drove Europeans out of their Latin American colonies. Once Spain and Portugal were defeated, the U.S. wanted to ensure that they did not reconquer their lost possessions. As a result, President Monroe instituted the Monroe Doctrine which stated that any attempts by European nations to regain their former colonies in the Western Hemisphere would be viewed as an act of war. This policy was illustrated in political cartoons which showed Uncle Sam armed and guarding over Latin America as European nations glared angrily in his direction from across a river representing the Atlantic Ocean. The cartoonist illustrated that European nations were angry over this policy and accurately showed these nations staying away from the Western Hemisphere. Although this was primarily because the British helped with the enforcement of the Monroe Doctrine (the U.S. was not powerful enough to enforce it alone), the result was the same. European nations had been expelled from many of their colonies in the Western Hemisphere, allowing the United States to become even more isolated (Doc. 4).

This trend of isolation changed dramatically at the end of the 19th century. Following the Spanish-American War, the United States gained several colonies including the Philippines and Puerto Rico. The United States also began to become more involved in Chinas through the Open Door policy and American's desire to obtain more trade opportunities, especially in light of the fear that the American frontier had closed. The United States would continue to participate in foreign events, most notably, the First World War, in which President Wilson claimed the United States would make the world safe for democracy. It was not until the end of this war that the United States would return to isolation.

Exercise 30: Comprehensive DBQ Analysis 3

Document 1: Speech

"The constitution contains no express provisions respecting slavery in a new state that may be admitted into the union: every regulation upon this subject, belongs to the power whose consent is necessary to the formation and admission of such state. Congress may therefore make it a condition of the admission of a new state, that slavery shall be forever prohibited within the same. We may with the more confidence pronounce this to be the true construction of the constitution, as it has been so amply confirmed by the past decisions of Congress."

— Rufus King, *The Substance of Two Speeches...In Response to the Missouri Bill,* 1819

Directions: Fill out the grid below to identify the most important aspects of the speech. Being able to describe the information in the speech is critical to your DBQ response.

MEET THE DOCUMENT.		
Type *(check all that apply)*		
☐ Letter	☐ Report	☐ Newspaper
☐ Advertisement	☐ Memorandum	☐ Congressional document
☐ Chart or Table	☐ Speech	☐ Other
☐ Court document	☐ Presidential document	_____

OBSERVE ITS PARTS.	
Who delivered it?	
Who read/received it? *(Audience)*	
When is it from? *(Historical Situation)*	
Where is it from? *(Historical Situation)*	

TRY TO MAKE SENSE OF IT.	
What is it talking about?	
Write one sentence summarizing the speech.	
Why was it written? *(Purpose or Point of View)*	
Quote evidence from the speech that illustrates your statement above.	
What was happening at the time in history this speech was written? *(Historical Situation)*	

USE IT AS HISTORICAL EVIDENCE.	
What did you find out from this speech that you might not learn anywhere else?	
What other documents or historical evidence are you going to use to help you understand this topic?	

Part 2: Write an Analytical Summary of the Document

_____

_____

_____

_____

_____

_____

_____

_____

_____

Document 2: Political Cartoon

— John L. Magee, *Forcing Slavery Down the Throat of a Freesoiler,* 1856

Part 1: Analyze the Political Cartoon

Directions: Fill out the grid below to identify the most important aspects of the cartoon.
Being able to describe the information depicted in the drawing is critical to your DBQ response.

MEET THE CARTOON.	
Quickly scan the cartoon. What do you notice first?	
What is the title or caption?	
OBSERVE ITS PARTS.	
Words: Are there labels, descriptions, thoughts, or dialogue?	
Visuals: List the people, objects, and places in the cartoon.	
Visuals: List the actions or activities being shown in the illustration.	
TRY TO MAKE SENSE OF IT.	
Words: Which words or phrases are the most significant?	
Words: What adjectives describe the emotions portrayed?	
Visuals: Which of the visuals are symbolic?	
Visuals: What do the symbols stand for?	
Who drew this cartoon/drawing?	

When is it from?	
What was happening at the time in history it was created? *(Historical Situation)*	
What is the message? List evidence from the cartoon that led you to your conclusion. *(Purpose or Point of View)*	
USE IT AS HISTORICAL EVIDENCE.	
What did you find out from this image that you might not learn anywhere else?	
What other documents or historical evidence are you going to use to help you understand this event or topic?	

Part 2: Write an Analytical Summary of the Document

_____

_____

_____

_____

_____

_____

_____

_____

_____

Document 3: Resolution

"Resolved, That all petitions, memorials, resolutions, propositions, or papers, relating in any way or to any extent whatever to the subject of slavery, or the abolition of slavery, shall, without being either printed or referred, be laid upon the table, and that no further action whatever shall be had thereon."

— Gag Rule/Pinckney Resolution 3, 1836

Part 1: Analyze the Text

Directions: Fill out the grid below to identify the most important aspects of the text.
Being able to describe the information in the document is critical to your DBQ response.

MEET THE DOCUMENT.		
Type *(check all that apply)*		
☐ Letter	☐ Report	☐ Newspaper
☐ Advertisement	☐ Memorandum	☐ Congressional document
☐ Chart or Table	☐ Speech	☐ Other
☐ Court document	☐ Presidential document	_____
OBSERVE ITS PARTS.		
Who wrote it?		
Who read/received it? *(Audience)*		
When is it from? *(Historical Situation)*		
Where is it from? *(Historical Situation)*		
TRY TO MAKE SENSE OF IT.		
What is it talking about?		
Write one sentence summarizing the document.		
Why was it written? *(Purpose or Point of View)*		
Quote evidence from the document that illustrates your statement above.		
What was happening at the time in history this document was written? *(Historical Situation)*		

USE IT AS HISTORICAL EVIDENCE.	
What did you find out from this document that you might not learn anywhere else?	
What other documents or historical evidence are you going to use to help you understand this event or topic?	

Part 2: Write an Analytical Summary of the Document

_____

_____

_____

_____

_____

_____

_____

_____

_____

Document 4: Supreme Court Decision

"Congress have no right to prohibit the citizens of any particular State or States from taking up their home there, while it permits citizens of other States to do so. Nor has it a right to give privileges to one class of citizens which it refuses to another. The territory is acquired for their equal and common benefit — and if open to any, it must be open to all upon equal and the same terms.

"Every citizen has a right to take with him into the Territory any article of property which the Constitution of the United States recognises as property.

"The act of Congress, therefore, prohibiting a citizen of the United States from taking with him his slaves when he removes to the Territory in question to reside, is an exercise of authority over private property which is not warranted by the Constitution — and the removal of the plaintiff, by his owner, to that Territory, gave him no title to freedom."

— Excerpt from Supreme Court Decision in *Dred Scott v. Sandford*, 1857

Part 1: Analyze the Text

Directions: Fill out the grid below to identify the most important aspects of the text.
Being able to describe the information in the document is critical to your DBQ response.

MEET THE DOCUMENT.		
Type *(check all that apply)*		
☐ Letter	☐ Report	☐ Newspaper
☐ Advertisement	☐ Memorandum	☐ Congressional document
☐ Chart or Table	☐ Speech	☐ Other
☐ Court document	☐ Presidential document	_____

OBSERVE ITS PARTS.	
Who wrote it?	
Who read/received it? *(Audience)*	
When is it from? *(Historical Situation)*	
Where is it from? *(Historical Situation)*	

TRY TO MAKE SENSE OF IT.	
What is it talking about?	
Write one sentence summarizing the document.	
Why was it written? *(Purpose or Point of View)*	
Quote evidence from the document that illustrates your statement above.	
What was happening at the time in history this document was written? *(Historical Situation)*	

USE IT AS HISTORICAL EVIDENCE.	
What did you find out from this document that you might not learn anywhere else?	
What other documents or historical evidence are you going to use to help you understand this event or topic?	

Part 2: Write an Analytical Summary of the Document

_____

_____

_____

_____

_____

_____

_____

_____

_____

Document 5: Position Paper

"The committee [of the South Carolina Legislature] have bestowed on the subjects referred to them the deliberate attention which their importance demands; and the result, on full investigation, is a unanimous opinion that the act of Congress of the last session, with the whole system of legislation imposing duties on imports, not for revenue, but the protection of one branch of industry at the expense of others, is unconstitutional, unequal, and oppressive, and calculated to corrupt the public virtue and destroy the liberty of the country; which propositions they propose to consider in the order stated, and then to conclude their report with the consideration of the important question of the remedy."

— John C. Calhoun, *South Carolina Exposition and Protest,* 1828

Part 1: Analyze the Text

Directions: Fill out the grid below to identify the most important aspects of the document. Being able to describe the information in the text is critical to your DBQ response.

MEET THE DOCUMENT.		
Type *(check all that apply)*		
☐ Letter	☐ Report	☐ Newspaper
☐ Advertisement	☐ Memorandum	☐ Congressional document
☐ Chart or Table	☐ Speech	☐ Other
☐ Court document	☐ Presidential document	_____

OBSERVE ITS PARTS.	
Who wrote it?	
Who read/received it? *(Audience)*	
When is it from? *(Historical Situation)*	
Where is it from? *(Historical Situation)*	

TRY TO MAKE SENSE OF IT.	
What is it talking about?	
Write one sentence summarizing the document.	
Why was it written? *(Purpose or Point of View)*	
Quote evidence from the document that illustrates your statement above.	
What was happening at the time in history this document was written? *(Historical Situation)*	

USE IT AS HISTORICAL EVIDENCE.	
What did you find out from this document that you might not learn anywhere else?	
What other documents or historical evidence are you going to use to help you understand this event or topic?	

Part 2: Write an Analytical Summary of the Document

_____

_____

_____

_____

_____

_____

_____

_____

_____

Document 6: Poster

CAUTION!!

COLORED PEOPLE

OF BOSTON, ONE & ALL,

You are hereby respectfully **CAUTIONED** and advised, to avoid conversing with the

Watchmen and Police Officers of Boston,

For since the recent **ORDER OF THE MAYOR & ALDERMEN,** they are empowered to act as

KIDNAPPERS

AND

Slave Catchers,

And they have already been actually employed in **KIDNAPPING, CATCHING, AND KEEPING SLAVES.** Therefore, if you value your **LIBERTY,** and the ***Welfare of the Fugitives*** among you, ***Shun*** them in every possible manner, as so many ***HOUNDS*** on the track of the most unfortunate of your race.

Keep a Sharp Look Out for KIDNAPPERS, and have TOP EYE open.

APRIL 24, 1851.

— Publication Date: 1851

Part 1: Analyze the Poster

Directions: Fill out the grid below to identify the most important aspects of the poster. Being able to describe the information conveyed in the poster is critical to your DBQ response.

MEET THE DOCUMENT.		
Type *(check all that apply)*		
☐ Letter	☐ Report	☐ Newspaper
☐ Advertisement	☐ Memorandum	☐ Congressional document
☐ Chart or Table	☐ Speech	☐ Other
☐ Court document	☐ Presidential document	_____
OBSERVE ITS PARTS.		
Who wrote it?		
Who read/received it? *(Audience)*		
When is it from? *(Historical Situation)*		
Where is it from? *(Historical Situation)*		
TRY TO MAKE SENSE OF IT.		
What is it talking about?		
Write one sentence summarizing the document.		
Why was it produced? *(Purpose or Point of View)*		
Quote evidence from the document that illustrates your statement above.		
What was happening at the time in history this document was created? *(Historical Situation)*		

USE IT AS HISTORICAL EVIDENCE.	
What did you find out from this document that you might not learn anywhere else?	
What other documents or historical evidence are you going to use to help you understand this event or topic?	

Part 2: Write an Analytical Summary of the Document

_____

_____

_____

_____

_____

_____

_____

_____

_____

_____

Document 7: Government Document

"In the present case, the fact is established with certainty. We assert, that fourteen of the states have deliberately refused for years past to fulfil their constitutional obligations....

"The states of...Massachusetts, Connecticut, Rhode Island...have enacted laws which either nullify the Acts of Congress or render useless any attempt to execute them....

"We therefore, the people of South Carolina...have solemnly declared that the Union herefore existing...is dissolved, and the State of South Carolina has resumed her position among the nations of the world as a separate and independent state."

— Christopher Memminger, *Declaration of the Immediate Causes Which Induce and Justify the Secession of South Carolina from the Federal Union,* 1860

Part 1: Analyze the Text

Directions: Fill out the grid below to identify the most important aspects of the document.
Being able to describe the information conveyed in the text is critical to your DBQ response.

MEET THE DOCUMENT.		
Type *(check all that apply)*		
☐ Letter	☐ Report	☐ Newspaper
☐ Advertisement	☐ Memorandum	☐ Congressional document
☐ Chart or Table	☐ Speech	☐ Other
☐ Court document	☐ Presidential document	_____

OBSERVE ITS PARTS.	
Who wrote it?	
Who read/received it? *(Audience)*	
When is it from? *(Historical Situation)*	
Where is it from? *(Historical Situation)*	

TRY TO MAKE SENSE OF IT.	
What is it talking about?	
Write one sentence summarizing the document.	
Why was it written? *(Purpose or Point of View)*	
Quote evidence from the document that illustrates your statement above.	
What was happening at the time in history this document was written? *(Historical Situation)*	

USE IT AS HISTORICAL EVIDENCE.	
What did you find out from this document that you might not learn anywhere else?	
What other documents or historical evidence are you going to use to help you understand this event or topic?	

Part 2: Write an Analytical Summary of the Document

_____

_____

_____

_____

_____

_____

_____

_____

_____

_____

Tying It All Together: DBQ Practice Question 3

Now that you have analyzed each document individually, it is time to put all of the information together in an organized and coherent essay. To practice this, respond to the prompt below. Include the information you summarized while analyzing each of the documents provided earlier in this section, as well as outside information you have learned in class or from a text.

DBQ 3 Prompt

Analyze why compromise was unsuccessful at resolving the issues that led to the Civil War.

Write a Comprehensive DBQ Response

_____

_____

_____

_____

_____

_____

_____

_____

_____

_____

_____

_____

_____

_____

_____

DBQ 3: Compare Your Response to a Sample Response

Compare your essay to the sample written below. Your essay does not need to be exactly the same to be written well. However, it should reflect several commonalities. If your essay seems similar in structure/organization, content/evidence, and analysis, you have answered the question well. If there are major differences in these areas, it would be beneficial to note what the differences are and determine if you your writing would be stronger by adopting a model that corresponds with the sample.

DBQ 3 Prompt

From 1819 to 1860, compromises were made to reduce sectional tension. Analyze why these compromises were unsuccessful at resolving the issues that led to the Civil War.

Sample Comprehensive DBQ Response

An early dispute over the legality of slavery was overcome by allowing individual state legislatures to determine whether slavery would be allowed. Additionally, the federal government implemented the Three-Fifths Compromise to alleviate disputes over the apportionment of representatives. In 1793, the first fugitive slave law was enacted to help Southern slave owners retain control of runaways who had escaped to the North. In virtually every early piece of federal legislation addressing the issue of slavery, Southern slave owners were placated. However, new issues would arise with the additional land acquisitions. Initially, when new territories became states, the sectional balance was maintained through compromise. Compromise was also successful at reducing sectional tensions created by economic policies. However, during the 1830s the government began avoiding the challenging conversations that slavery created. Conflict began to grow when the sectional balance could no longer be maintained, which led to earlier compromises failing when they were adjusted or ignored. Violence broke out both in states and the Senate chamber, showing that rational discourse and future compromises were unlikely. Finally, when the Supreme Court declared slavery was legal everywhere, the division between the North and

South was nearly complete. It would just take the election of President Lincoln and the formal declaration of secession by South Carolina to make the Civil War official.

Initially, the threat of sectional conflict was resolved through compromise. In 1819 Missouri requested admittance to the U.S. as a slave state. Northerners were concerned that this would give the South too much political strength in the Senate. This was highlighted when Northerners like Rufus King spoke against allowing Missouri to be a slave state. The substance of the speech was based on the unconstitutional nature of extending slavery which indicates that King was trying to use the supreme law of the land to prevent Missouri from becoming a slave state. King pointed out that the Constitution did not directly state how to handle the legality of slavery in new states and further pointed out that the Constitution did allow Congress to determine the expectations that must be met before a territory could be admitted as a state. King believed that Congress should include a stipulation that "outlawed slavery in Missouri (Doc. 1). King's rationale was not acted upon and instead, Congress passed the Missouri Compromise created by Henry Clay. This compromise allowed Missouri to be admitted as a slave state, but it also admitted Maine as a free state, preserving the sectional balance at the time. The rest of the Louisiana Purchase was to be divided at 36°30' to avoid future conflicts over slavery in the territory.

New divisions within the nation emerged over economic policy; however, this division also was solved through compromise. Before John Quincy Adams left the presidency, he strengthened the American System by implementing a high protective tariff, the Tariff of 1828. Southerners were outraged at the increased cost this tariff would create for them and referred to it as the Tariff of Abominations. In response, John C. Calhoun wrote the South Carolina Exposition. Calhoun's intention was to increase opposition to the tariff as well as to promote the doctrine of He argued that the tariff was unconstitutional since Congress created an unequal policy to benefit one section of that nation at the expense of another. Calhoun continued to by stating that the tariff was oppressive and could destroy American freedoms (Doc. 5). The Exposition encouraged the state legislature of South Carolina to nullify the tariff. The incoming president, Andrew Jackson, was not a strong supporter of the tariff; however, he would not allow federal power (his power) to be challenged. As a result, the nullification crisis occurred which was marked by the potential of fighting between the U.S. military and the South Carolina militia. However, Henry Clay was able to solve this conflict through a compromise, the Compromise Tariff of 1833 which maintained the tariff but lowered the duty assessed on foreign goods.

It became more difficult to find resolutions to the issue of slavery when Congress began restricting discussions on abolition. During this time, the Second Great Awakening had led many Americans to become involved in a reform movement. Some of these reformers supported the cause of abolition. As a result, they desired that bills addressing abolition be addressed in Congress. However, since this was an extremely volatile subject, Congress passed the gag resolutions. This demanded that all petitions, resolutions, or propositions that dealt with the subject of slavery set aside instead of being discussed or voted upon. This ensured that nothing could occur dealing with issues regarding slavery. This rule was to ignore the very issue that was beginning to divide the nation (Doc. 3).

After the Mexican War, the sectional balance was not maintained; this ended the ability for compromises to reduce tension. After the war, the U.S. gained a huge amount of land from Mexico. As a result, the government needed to determine if slavery would be allowed in the new territories. Henry Clay, Daniel Webster, and John C. Calhoun supported the Compromise of 1850. This allowed California to be a free state, but all of the other territories would make the decisions through popular sovereignty. The compromise also enacted a stricter Fugitive Slave Law. This made it easier for slaves who had successfully escaped to Northern states to be returned to their masters. Northerners were outraged at the violation of their states' rights, and a poster from the era underscores their desire to challenge the law. It warned Black people "one and all" of "conversing with the watchmen and police" who were attempting to catch runaway slaves and capture free Black people to take them to the South to be enslaved. Little distinction was made by the slavecatchers between free Black people and fugitives, and so both groups were cautioned that their liberty was at stake if they should be caught by these men whom Northerners viewed as kidnappers. The abolitionists believed that free Black people should be treated with respect rather than being hunted down by slavecatchers, whom they referred to as "hounds" in a poster from the era (Doc. 6). In addition to warning Black people, abolitionists provided legal assistance and, in some cases, broke the accused out of captivity and helped them gain passage to Canada. By the North gaining more free territories and the South having a stronger Fugitive Slave Law, tensions between the two regions could not be resolved as in the past.

When previous compromises were adjusted, violence occurred. Senator Stephen Douglas did not want a railroad to be built through the South as had been planned. Douglas realized the railroad would bring wealth wherever it passed, so he brokered the Kansas-Nebraska Act. This compromise allowed the railroad to be built in the North, and in return, the Nebraska territory would be divided, and slavery would be determined by popular sovereignty. This broke the Missouri Compromise. A cartoon drawn at the time shows a free-soil point of view that slavery was being forced down their throats and that this type of action may spread from Kansas to other places like Cuba. The cartoon also illustrated the immorality of slavery because it led to the death of enslaved people and the breakup of families (Doc. 2). In response to the Kansas-Nebraska Act, violence broke out through a statewide civil war. Violence also broke out on the Senate floor following Charles Sumner's Crimes Against Kansas speech. A cartoon illustrates congressman Preston Brooks caning Sumner as other pro-slavery politicians cheer him on and hold back those who may have helped Sumner. The point of view of the cartoonist was shown through the sarcastic reference to Southern chivalry; unable to make a coherent argument through the use of the pen, they would resort to using a club. This action also showed that Congress was no longer capable of making compromises successfully.

The conflict became even worse when previous compromises were nullified. Dred Scott, a slave who had been moved to free-soil territories, believed that he should have been granted his freedom. However, when his case was heard by the Supreme Court, it was decided that he was to remain a slave. The Court felt that preventing slave owners from entering a territory with their slaves would have denied them the freedom of movement offered to non-slaveholders. Therefore, anyone who wanted to move to the territory should be able to, without condition. The Court further stated that "Every citizen has the right to take...into the Territory any article of property"; therefore, slave owners must be allowed to take their slaves into any territory (Doc. 4). The purpose of this decision was to resolve future arguments over free and slave soil by basing the decision on the Constitution. Although the goal was to avoid future conflict, this only exacerbated the issue and Northerners gave up any pretense of following the Fugitive Slave Law.

All efforts to maintain peaceful compromise ended with Lincoln's election. Lincoln had run on a free-soil platform in direct contrast to the Dred Scott v. Sandford decision. Although Lincoln was focused on Western lands, Southern states felt that his election was a threat to all slave owners. As a result, South Carolina seceded from the Union after Lincoln's election, pointing out that Northern states were not following the Fugitive Slave Act and were acting outside of the Constitution. South Carolina seceded when its government "solemnly declared that the Union herefore existing...is dissolved" and declared that it was a nation unto itself (Doc. 7).

After the Civil War, tension remained high between the federal government and Southern states. The radical Republicans in the federal government passed the Reconstruction Amendments, which were designed to protect the freedmen. However, the redeemer state governments of the South attempted to prevent the freedmen from exercising their newly acquired freedoms. Additionally, the Ku Klux Klan originated during this time as a terrorist organization designed to intimidate freedmen into accepting a subservient status. In response, the federal government passed the Force Acts, establishing a period of military rule in the South. The federal government was able to assist the freedmen when they were uncompromising in their support. However, the election of 1876 led to the Compromise of 1877. At this point, the Republicans in the federal government ended the Force Act, ended Reconstruction, and gained a president at the expense of the Black population of the South.

Afterword

TAKING THE AP U.S. HISTORY COURSE AND THE APUSH EXAM is a challenging undertaking. We commend you on your ambition and perseverance. We hope that this book has helped you sharpen your writing skills by increasing your familiarity with the kinds of prompts you will encounter on the exam and the style of writing that is rewarded by AP readers. Practicing that style of historical writing through the exercises in this book should give you the confidence you need to succeed on the APUSH exam. For more help with your APUSH studies, we invite you to explore our other study materials:

AP U.S. History Exam Prep Guide and Course Reader

APUSH Pocket Dictionary

Our resources are designed to help you succeed...in a hurry! Find them on Amazon or at https://stampedelearning.com.

From all of us at Stampede Learning Systems, we wish you luck on the APUSH exam, and we hope you will continue to seek out challenging classes as you continue your education.

Made in the USA
Las Vegas, NV
05 November 2021

33796005R00136